Reviews :

"I couldn't put the thing down – it took me all of two evenings to read, and the amount of times I dropped it on my face would almost be constituted as self-harm. The humility and honesty within these pages is something I found most moving. The cutting rawness is a stroke of genius and is incredibly emotive – I consider myself to be fairly tight-lipped and I most definitely had to take a few moments to gather myself at points. As a Christian, there were always going to be parts that challenged me, and in a way, that's what I love about faith in whatever form it presents itself. The prophetic ministry is something that has developed quite naturally, and much like Derek, I can only be honest and say that it simply isn't me but Him. I'm sure you'll find this read insightful and poignant at whatever stage of life it finds you, and remember: the experiences you have in pursuit of understanding this world, and the next, can never be taken away from you. God bless."

Josh Charman, Co-Founder of Oaza Nadziei.

Together with my husband Eric I met Derek Moore over ten years ago when we joined a Spiritual Development Group he had established once a week in Lampeter, West Wales. It was with great delight that I was given the opportunity to learn more about Derek and the journey he has taken through his life and he has shared with us in his Autobiography. It tells the story of one man's journey looking for answers to questions and seeking out the truth of his own existence as he travels along the pathway of life.

Sharon K Bingham.

Derek Moore is a nice ordinary bloke, the office jobs of his early life show him on a journey through a normal, some would say unremarkable, journey of work promotions and relationships settling down.

One day though, a spiritualist medium told him something about himself that even he didn't know and his whole life changed forever.

In this book you will find stories that seem to defy any other explanation than this; Derek has a way of communicating with the spirit of people no longer living. His integrity and painstaking ability to reveal his thoroughly down-to-earth and infinitely sane way of being in the world leave us without doubt, that this is an honest man exploring what is happening to him with absolutely no sleight of hand.

I came to this book as a complete sceptic about 'life after death' but after reading it, I know there are things that have happened to Derek that cannot easily be explained away. Derek Moore is the genuine article and this is his remarkable story.

Maj Ikle.

A Part of Our Life

(A spiritual biography)

by
A Part of God
(Derek Moore)

Published by Cowry Publishing
Gwisgo Ltd, 8 Sgwar Alban, Aberaeron,
Ceredigion, SA46 0AD Wales, UK

www.cowrypublishing.co.uk

First published in May 2018

The right of Derek Moore to be identified as the author of this work has been asserted by him in accordance with the Copyright, Designs and Patents Act of 1988.
Copyright ©2018 Derek Moore.
Printed and bound in Ceredigion by Gomer Press
Cover design: Karen Gemma Brewer
Cover image: Coral Polge

A CIP catalogue record for this book is
available from the British Library

ISBN 978-1-908146-02-1

All rights reserved. No part of this publication may be reproduced, stored in a retrieval system or transmitted in any form or by any means, electronic, mechanical, photocopying, recording or otherwise without the prior written permission of the publishers. This book may not be lent, hired out, resold or otherwise disposed of by way of trade in any form of binding or cover other than that in which it is published, without the prior consent of the publishers.

Acknowledgements are due:

Especially to:
My wife Frances, who always supported, encouraged and loved me with total loyalty. I think of her every day and will love her eternally;

Pat, Elen, Sue, Richard, Kay, Carol, Neil and others that have been a part of my spiritual journey;

Those unseen: Golden Eagle, Habude, Nick, Steven and all that came in the early stages of my development;

Coral Polge for pictures of Habude, Golden Eagle, White Feather, Two Rivers and Andy's Grandfather Joseph and to Shirley Marlow for picture of Nicolai.

Lampeter Writers' Workshop, Maj for her writing classes, and Karen who has edited this book with great craft, making sure the context of statements have not been changed and the text remains in my voice. I must point out that, at my request, the verses within this book have not been edited;

My brother-in-law Andy and dear sister Lesley, without whose love this book would not have been published;

My step family Andrew, Stuart, Bernie and Eddie for always accepting me for who I am and making me a part of their lives;

Barry, Karen, Chris, Jan, Nick, Louise, Conny and Werner, true friends whose generosity and love to Frances and I, when we really needed help, I will never be able to repay.

I have not put deceased next to those who no longer grace this earth as I know they live on forever.

Introduction

I suppose for someone who doesn't read books, writing one may seem a strange thing to do. I have thought for many years now that when a book is written based on fact, philosophy or for that matter conjecture, the only person that knows how the words are meant to be interpreted is the writer themselves. This has led to my belief that readers of such books should ponder the contents deeply, and if accepting the whole or part of the text then this becomes their truth. Subsequently if it turns out to be wrong they cannot blame the author because they were wrong in their acceptance of it.

Why am I writing? Firstly I have felt impelled to do so for at least three years; and it is helping me get off my fat backside and do something practical with what is left of my earthly existence, although ironically I'm sitting on that same fat backside as I type. Secondly it is a reminder of the remarkable experiences which, at the age of 35, changed my thinking, and therefore changed me as a person and the life that followed; and in hope that more growth, knowledge and understanding may come to me as I lay down my story.

There are a few things to clarify before I start. In most cases I am using first names only of those people who have shared the 62 years of this life with me, except for the names of one family which I have changed completely. This book is not for the purpose of derogatory comment about others, so only content necessary to the relevance of my story is included. This book is not about religion although religions are an integral part of my story, especially Spiritualism which was the catalyst for the changes both internally and externally in me as a person. I try to write with complete truth. When spoken word is revealed I try to write the actual words that were used, to the best that my memory allows, which means that bad language is included, but if the words do differ I ensure that the context is true to the statements made.

The point of my story is the learning processes which sometimes may be overshadowed by the actual events, but it is these lessons that I hope may be taken from this book, although as with all aspects of life each individual has the right to interpret as they wish. I hope that by the end the reader will understand the title and authorship given.

To understand the great changes that occur you must first get to know who I was, and with that in mind I think the best place to start is at the beginning.

Chapter One: Childhood

In the time it took for my small fragile body to be launched 15 feet into the air, the short seven years of my life passed before my eyes...

Hi, my name is Derek Moore and I was born a child of the spirit on the 4th July 1954 in my maternal grandmother's house in Cosham, an outlying suburb of Portsmouth. I had two older brothers, Peter born 21st June 1947 and David born 4th April 1951. My sister Lesley Ann was to follow me four years later on 13th December 1958.

Father, Arthur Charles born 19th January 1921, was an aircraft fitter at the time of my birth, but in 1958 got a position as an estimator for the large electronics company G.E.C. (later to become Marconi Space and Development Systems). He worked for this company until retirement, becoming company chief estimator in 1979, and being awarded an MBE for services to exports. Mother, Joan Louisa born 24th August 1917, had nursed during the Second World War, and as we children grew older she would returned part-time to this profession until problems with her hands meant she could no longer work.

For the first three years of my life, we lived in Paulsgrove, a council estate built on the slope of Portsdown Hill. There were a lot of flat roof pre-fabricated homes which had been built in Portsmouth to house people after the end of the Second World War, but we were lucky enough to have a modest three bedroom house right at the summit of the building area. My only recollection of this time was being pecked by next door's chickens and running to mum sobbing with blood covering my fingertips. At the beginning of 1958 we moved to a semi-detached three bedroom house at the bottom of the hill very close to my maternal grandmother's house in Cosham. I was told later this was because the family doctor had told my father that he must get my mother off of the hill due to a slight heart condition. It was in December that year that my sister Lesley was born. My parents lived in this house for the rest of their days.

Dad was a hard working man with very strict moral values, and was definitely the head of the household. From the moment I started school at the age of five, I had to join my brothers Peter and David attending Sunday School each week at a small free church in Cosham. We were each given two or three old pennies to put into the collection, but most weeks only half of it would reach the collection plate as we would buy four blackjacks or a penny gobstopper to ease the pain of this weekly trial.

Sundays now seem a very significant memory of those childhood years, as I don't remember there being any real variation in them for the first 15 years of my life. I would get up for breakfast at about 9.30am, bacon, eggs, tomatoes and fried bread, all cooked by dad. Dinner would be at 1pm, lovely roast beef or pork with crispy roast potatoes spoiled only by the pile of horrible vegetables I would be encouraged to eat. This encouragement rarely succeeded and I remember on the odd occasion it did, I would soak the cabbage in vinegar to force it down and swallow the peas whole. My skin got so bad that my parents thought I might be developing scurvy so they took me to the family doctor and he gave them two options, put me on Vitamin C tablets or buy Ribena blackcurrant juice for me to drink. My dad said I wasn't going to have the pleasure of Ribena or I would never eat vegetables, so I ended up with the tablets. Off to church in the afternoon and then back home to sandwiches and cake. My father was a big man and it followed that our portion sizes were large also. This probably is the underlying cause of my undoubted obesity, and now I've come to love most vegetables my portion sizes have become even bigger. The only change to this Sunday ritual was on really sunny days, when we were all taken to the beach or Lido with a picnic.

From my memories of those early years only three are relevant to my story. The first was when at the age of six I decided to help my mother carry the milk bottles in from the doorstep. As I picked up the bottle I tripped and dropped it onto the step, falling on top of the broken glass. This meant a trip to the hospital and several stitches in both knees with the promise of a lollipop from the nurse if I was a brave boy. Needless to say there were no tears and I left the hospital with my gob full of lolly. This was to be repeated a few weeks later when I went to have the stitches taken out.

The second is a very faded memory of visiting an elderly couple in, what seemed to me, an old Victorian house in Reading. Sometimes it would be just me and mum travelling up by train and then, when dad got his first car, we would drive and I think Lesley would go with us. I remember inside the house seemed very dark and full of brown furniture. These visits were very formal and as children we sat at a table in the drawing room and were given tea and cake, but only spoke when spoken to. I must say that Peter's memory is somewhat different and whenever he went he enjoyed himself.

The significance of these two memories will come to light later in my story.

The third was about a year later during the summer holidays when my cousin Chrissie came over to play with us in the garden and suggested going to our local swing park. Chrissie lived with my Uncle Percy and Aunt Sylvia in my Nanas house which was in the next avenue to ours. She was 14, the same age as Peter and they both seemed so grown up to me, although she went everywhere barefoot and was considered a bit of a rebel.

I rushed in from the garden to ask my mother...

"Can me and David go to the swing park if Pete and Chrissie take us?"

"Yes, but only to the park. Don't go anywhere else and be home for lunch."

The swing park was about half a mile away and we only had to cross one minor road to get there.

We were all playing happily on the swings, slide and

roundabout when David shouted...

"Let's go to the creek to catch some crabs."

I had never caught crabs before and come to think of it I have never caught any sort of crabs since.

"Mum said we were not to go anywhere else but here," I insisted.

David was ten, he and I already had a somewhat competitive relationship and he would tease and goad me at every opportunity. I would consider it a great victory if I could get him into trouble. Sometimes the rivalry would get physical and then I would usually be left in tears.

"Don't be such a squinny," Dave yelled at me and set off hotfoot towards the creek, hastily followed by Chrissie and me. Pete tried to stop us, but to no avail and angrily stated that he was fed-up with us always getting him into strife and so was going home. Poor Peter, always left in charge of two younger brothers who took no notice of anything he said.

To reach the creek we had to cross a main road where the speed limit was 70 miles an hour. As we stood by the roadside close to a bend Dave turned to me and whispered...

"I'll beat you across the road."

I thought he meant right at that moment, so I rushed out into the road and was hit by a Renault Dolphin as it came round the bend. In the time it took for my small fragile body to be launched 15 feet into the air, the short seven years of my life passed before my eyes. It was as if every memory of my short life had been unlocked and was being played back for me like a black and white movie on fast forward. Seven years of life re-lived in the three seconds it took my body to rise and then drop to the hard road surface below, minus one wellington boot which had flown from my foot into the murky water. The car had swerved across the opposite stream of traffic and stopped inches before it would have crashed through a wire mesh fence and followed my boot into the water. The driver was a Naval Commander, on his way back to Brighton with his wife, daughter and her new born baby. My actions could have had very dire consequences, a thought which only really hit home in later life.

I jumped up from the road and ran to Chrissie, leaping into her arms, whilst the driver reversed to a safe place and came to see what state I was in. He put me in the back seat, took directions from Chrissie and drove me back home. Chrissie and Dave had got there before us and as we drove up the avenue I could see mum waiting by the front gate. I thought she looked angry. As I got out of the car and she came towards me, I ran in the opposite direction, nearly getting run over by the milk float as it made its daily deliveries. When she eventually caught me she just hugged and cuddled me. The look I had mistaken for anger was a look of shock and worry. The Commander took us both to the hospital where a doctor checked me over and told me how lucky I had been as I just had bruises and grazes on my hands and legs. He told mum to keep me warm and in bed for a few days in case of delayed shock. When dad came home that evening he hit the roof, although most of his anger was a release of thoughts of what could have been the outcome.

It must have been nearly two years later when we were all in the living room one evening, dad in his chair reading the local evening newspaper, mum sitting engrossed in one of her many Mills and Boon paperbacks (I think dad thought they were slightly pornographic), Peter and Lesley sitting on the sofa watching TV and Dave and I playing draughts on the floor. David was winning and couldn't help goading me and being smug every time he jumped one of my pieces. To this day I don't know why I said what I did; I don't even remember thinking before I spoke...

"If you hadn't said I'll beat you across the road I wouldn't have got run over."

Oops!

My father slowly lowered the paper down to his lap and quietly said, "What did you just say?"

I repeated my statement and David's backside felt the full force of my dad's considerably large hand. I'm not sure he ever forgave me for that, although I will point out that he certainly got recompense on more than one occasion.

Throughout these early years as with most children, my personality and relationship with my family was being formed. My brothers and I were never that close, just competitive, or at least that's how it seemed to me. I am sorry to say I began to pass down the constant teasing to my sister who, with three boys as brothers, was always going to end up as a tomboy. I would constantly use her as my goal keeper or make her bowl balls down to me which I would hit for miles with the cricket bat and then send her off to fetch, only so I could hit the next ball for six and send her off again.

Mother was to me a very caring lady and loyal wife to dad. She was always there with the iodine to heal our grazed knees, and a cuddle whenever tears flowed. Most of the time there was home cooked food on the table, although we were subjected to periods when school dinners were the order of the day. I hated those days and would give mine away to classmates or the bullies of the school. Not because I was scared of them, just that I never liked the look of what was being offered as the main part of the meal. I did however love the old style puddings, spotted dick, jam roly poly, or my favourite, queen of puddings. I also loved the thick custard and would fill my stomach with these puddings to quell any hunger pangs. Sometimes I would keep the school dinner money, go to the chippie at lunch break and buy sausage and chips until the money ran out and for the last two days of the week I'd have to wait until tea time before I ate.

Dad strived to support us all. A straight talking, honest man with stringent views of how life should be, how you had to work hard to provide even the most basic of needs for your family. Unfortunately, this need to support and nurture would result in his view being the only view, as any attempt to contradict would be shouted down. He would only vote Tory and would vehemently defend their values. I later learned that mum had different views on many subjects, but had decided to keep her own counsel as she realised there was very little point in stating them outwardly. Dad's strict values quite often bought times when black clouds would descend over the household. One day all would be happy and bright and then he would come home from work and tell everyone to leave him alone. He wouldn't speak or answer to anyone and acted as if his whole world had collapsed around him. These dark moods were nearly always brought on by pressures he felt in work, and they would sometimes last for weeks until the job he was involved with had finished and his burden released. These times were hard on all of us and my mother would sometimes open the kitchen window and scream to release her tension. I remember my father walking out one evening in a black mood and a vase from the window sill suddenly flying past my head. My mother wasn't aiming it at me it was just a desperate attempt to rid her-self of days of frustration and being treated like shit. I have to say now that dad would never strike out during these moods, he would just isolate himself and seem to exist in his own world of despair.

 In between these cloudy periods things were fine and on Saturday afternoons when Pompey were playing at home he would take Les and me to Fratton Park to watch the match. He had first taken me when I was six and wouldn't let me go to the child's turnstile, quite willing to pay full price for me so that I was always with him. But nearly every time, the man would tell him to lift me over the turnstile and I would get in for free. When Lesley started coming he would let me take her to the children's entrance and meet us on the other side. I suppose I was about ten then and he trusted me to look after her. I continued to go until I was 26 when an away trip to Crystal Palace with a friend resulted in a frightening experience. Palace fans chased us away from our coach and we nearly ended up crushed against a wall as everyone barged past. My friend fell and was stamped on and had a large cut down one of his legs. That was enough for me and I have never been to a football match live since; TV only from then on. I was also a great Manchester United supporter and idolised Georgie Best, who even my dad said was the best footballer he had ever seen. I learnt all about their history from the early days of Newton Heath through to the terrible Munich air disaster, and when they finally won the European Cup in 1968 I remember feeling more elated than I had in 1966 when England won the World Cup. Every now and then we would also go to the local cricket ground for a day out watching Hampshire play, so as you can see there were plenty of good times to counteract the bad.

Christmas day in our house was always fun. We children would be in bouncing on mum and dad's bed by about 5am in the morning, and around six we would go downstairs to where our presents were all laid out on the living room chairs. We would only have perhaps six or seven things to open, the largest, price wise, being from mum and dad and this was worth about a fiver. It wasn't like it is today; dad would never have gone into debt buying presents he couldn't really afford. I remember one year he had gone to Bobby Tambling's sports shop in Havant and my present was a pair of George Best football boots. I was the only one in the school team to have them, and in those days they were quite unique as they were purple and laced up on the side of the boot. It wasn't long before more pairs turned up in the changing rooms.

Every Boxing Day evening there would be a big family get together at my paternal grandmother's house in Baileys Road in Portsmouth. She would only answer to Gran and you would get a stern rebuke if you called her Nan or Nana. My dad was one of eight children who all married and had children of their own, apart from my uncle Bill who died at a relatively young age and of whom I have no clear memory. On my father's side were his younger brothers Ben and David and sisters Ethel, Violet, Joyce and Peggy. On my mother's side there were just her brothers, Percy and Wilfred. Both my grandfathers had passed, my mum's father had apparently been run over by a horse and cart in Reading before I was born, and dad's dad had passed when I was three years old so I had no memory of him either. On these Boxing Day evenings everybody appeared to have a great time, but I always found myself standing in a corner somewhere feeling shy and uncomfortable when any of the adults spoke to me or tried to get me to join in with the festivities. Small red headed child with no real confidence unless he had a ball in his hand or at his feet, and no art of conversation or any opinion on any subject unless it was football or cricket. This may have been due to the restrictive nature of my home life although Peter and David seemed to interact ok, but Lesley appeared to suffer the same feelings of inadequacy that I did. These environments, along with my school days, were to mould my personality for the first 32 years of my life.

Chapter Two: School Years

"Look out sir. Sydney's about to fall on your head"...

I started school at the age of five at Wymering Infant and Junior school about a quarter of a mile from home. On my first day our teacher, Miss Wheat, had been telling us a story whilst rocking her chair back and forth when suddenly she rocked too hard and went backwards ending up sprawled on the floor with her legs in the air. There was a classroom full of five year olds in hysterics. I have never forgotten that day, nor my first ever school dinner. I was given mashed up swede and made to eat it. After one mouthful I was violently sick all over the table and unfortunately all over the poor little girl sitting next to me. I think I remember shouting at the teacher...

"I told you I didn't like it", as the tears ran down my face and embarrassment set in and with the little girl screaming, traumatised beside me.

 The rest of those early days are a bit of a blur, until the fourth year of junior school when my father decided that a mixed school was not good for me and moved me to Portsdown Secondary Modern School for boys. This again was about a five minute walk from home and is where the rest of my schooling took place.

I loved my sports and was pretty good at most. Anything that involved striking or kicking a ball was a definite hit in my eyes, especially football and cricket. I captained the school cricket teams at junior level and was vice captain when a senior. I also played cricket for Portsmouth boys at senior level. My dad never watched me play cricket and I can only remember him coming to one football match, after which he said...

"You did ok son," and that was the end of that.

It was about this time that the school decided to introduce swimming lessons and once a week we were taken to the local baths. When you could complete a width of the pool you would be told that the following week you had to attempt your 25 yard swim for which you would receive a certificate.

When I was told this it frightened me as you had to start the swim at the far end of the pool which was about 12 feet deep. I went home that evening with this fear and worried about it all week until the evening before the next visit to the pool when I suddenly burst into tears.

"What's up with you, why are you crying?" Dad enquired.

"I've got to do my 25 yard swim tomorrow and I'm scared of the deep end," I blubbed.

"Don't be such a coward, just get in there and get on with it, and for god's sake stop whingeing," he snapped.

That was it, no empathy for a small boy's fears, no encouragement.

The following day I conquered my fear, completed the swim, gained my certificate, took it home and put it in a drawer in my bedroom. Dad never asked if I had completed it and I felt that if he didn't care, there was no point in showing him.

It was strange really because on other occasions he did show that he cared. I remember being sent to bed early for some reason or other when I about eight. I can't remember what I had done wrong but my dad didn't punish you without cause so I must have deserved it. At bedtimes we would undress and leave our clothes on chairs in the kitchen ready to dress for school the following morning. I was in my room sulking and feeling very hard done by, when it suddenly came into my head that I should run away. I crept downstairs at about eight o'clock, pulled the kitchen door shut and quietly began to put my clothes on. Suddenly the door opened and there stood Dad...

"What do you think you're doing?" he asked in a gentle tone.

"I'm running away" I answered in a trembling voice, my eyes beginning to well up.

"Who are you running away from?"

"You," I replied

"Why?"

"Because you're mean to me and I don't like it here anymore."

"Where are you going?"

"Don't know."

He walked over to the kettle and began filling it...

"Have you got some money for your bus fare? You'll need some to buy food. Shall I make you some sandwiches to take with you?"

By now the tears were in full flow and I didn't know what else to say. He came over, picked me up and sat me on his lap.

"Want a piece of bread pudding and come in the living room for half an hour before you go?"

"Yes."

"Put your pyjamas back on first then, it's a cold night out there, be much better to go in the morning."

So it was bread pudding sitting on his lap, then back to bed and school in the morning, everything back to normal.

I was usually in the top five of my class so when I failed the 11 plus exam, I could feel my father's disappointment as that meant that none of his boys were to be Grammar school pupils. I can't say I failed on purpose, but I do remember that I didn't want to leave my friends and teammates and have to start again. My sister was to make up for us boys by passing the exam and going to the Northern Grammar School in Portsmouth. Lesley studied hard, not only for herself but because she didn't want to let her dad down. I think she felt pressure to do well in order to please him.

A few weeks before I moved to the senior school my mother came to my bedroom to tell me that my Nan had gone to join the angels in heaven, the first time in my life that I experienced real grief. I loved my Nan although Lesley says she frightened her, and Chrissie who lived in the same house says that Nan didn't like her and never spoke to her. It seems strange that I loved this lady that others seemed scared of, and I remember my mother holding me close as we wept together.

Senior School was not an unpleasant experience for me mainly because I was good at sports and played alongside those considered as hard nuts and bullies. I didn't really suffer from any bullying, in fact if somebody started on me I had many teammates to come to my rescue. I don't think it was the same for my brothers and believe they both suffered from bullying at some time during their school years. Dad had a habit of coming home from work, looking at you and then taking a half-crown (twelve and a half pence in today's money) from his pocket and telling you to go to the barbers after school the next day and get a haircut. Short back and sides was the only acceptable style. I was also the only boy to go to the first year seniors still wearing short trousers, so took a lot of teasing 'til dad relented and got me my first long pair. School and home life only mixed in the form of homework. When I got home and had eaten dinner I had to sit in the kitchen and complete whatever tasks had been set for that day, and polish my shoes, before I could go out or watch television. We didn't get a television until 1966 when dad bought one to watch the World Cup, so I would sneak off to Nanas to watch. We had very strict bedtimes in those early years, six o'clock until we were about eight, then probably seven or seven thirty up to the age of twelve, and nine o'clock up to leaving school. I don't remember ever having school friends in the house at any time, young children running amok would not have been my father's cup of tea.

I was quite a good and obedient pupil but the swish of the cane did meet my hands on more than one occasion. Our history teacher Mr Lilywhite had a habit of leaving the room for a few minutes and we would take the opportunity to grab one person and remove their shoe to throw at him as he re-entered the room. It was never the same person twice and never the person who threw the shoe who got punished as the shoe was the only evidence, and therefore he would always cane the boy whose shoe it was. On one occasion he had pinned a large map of Australia to the blackboard and as he stood in front of it talking to us I suddenly had the urge to shout out,

"Look out sir Sydney's about to fall on your head."

He ducked and the whole class just fell about laughing. I wasn't laughing a few seconds later as the cane hit each of my hands twice in rapid succession. You didn't dare cry as you would have been teased relentlessly, and anyway it never hurt as much as my dad's large hand coming down across my backside when I had done something wrong. I think the worst punishment I had was from our science master, Mr Evans, who we nicknamed Fossil. He was teaching us one day and the boy sitting opposite kept whispering my name trying to get my attention,

"Derek...Derek...Derek...Der"...

"Fucking shut up you prat."

Mr Evans heard and had an invitation for me...

"What did you say Moore? Come out to the front and repeat it."

Oh shit!

"I was just telling Hibbard to keep quiet sir" I said fully expecting the cane to appear from behind the desk.

"I want 2,000 words on the pollination of flowers on my desk by nine o'clock tomorrow morning."

What the hell did I know about the pollination of flowers? It took me hours of research, and my dad laughed which did nothing to ease my pain although if he had known I had used the F- word in class my backside would have been sore. Why couldn't Fossil have just caned me?

We also had one sadistic teacher who would produce two canes, one short and quite thick and the other long and thin.

He called them Pinky and Perky and would ask you which one you wanted to be struck with, and it always surprised me when my classmates would choose the thin one which had far more whip and must have hurt far more than the thick one. Luckily I never had to choose.

So, school was going quite well and I had joined the drama group run by the school librarian whose name I can't remember. We used to put on a couple of shows a year in the main assembly hall and they always seemed to go down well with both teachers and pupils. I enjoyed the challenge and didn't mind staying behind after lessons to rehearse. English was my favourite of all the academic studies, especially making up stories and writing essays. I had a vivid imagination which might well have been stirred by those early bedtimes imposed at home. I would spend hours lying in bed inventing stories inspired by TV programmes and the films we had seen at Saturday morning pictures. Nearly every Saturday we would go to the local Odeon cinema, pay our sixpence and watch cartoons followed by a feature length film, Lassie, Lone Ranger or such like. Of course, in my day dreaming I was always the hero righting wrongs, shooting savage redskins or saving those I loved from some impending disaster. It was very seldom that I was asleep before midnight, and it was many years before I realised that the savages I was shooting were some of the most ill-treated human beings in history.

At home dad had been promoted to chief estimator in charge of an office of about 20 people pricing, and trying to win, multi million pound contracts for the company. Mum had started working part-time, Friday, Saturday and Sunday evenings, in charge of a ward at the Royal Hospital in the town centre. Peter had left school and taken an electrical fitter's apprenticeship in Portsmouth dockyard. David followed suit, but had chosen to be a fitter and turner, and I was studying for my C.S E's (Certificate of Secondary Education) in four subjects; English, Maths, Science and Technical Drawing. Also, the school had decided to run an electrical course and I had chosen to be a part of this so was being taught the basics in electrical engineering. I had only really chosen this to get out of what was aptly called Handyman's lessons, which involved digging the school's garden, weeding and planting which I found boring and too much like hard manual labour. My friend Barry and I would try every trick in the book to get out of Handyman's and one time after Religious Education, Mr Skews the teacher, a large jolly man who had come as a temp to teach Divinity, stated that he needed to go into Cosham to get something for his dinner that evening.

"Me and Eamsie will go for you sir," I said, Eames being Barry's surname.

"Ok I'll let Mr Austin know you won't be in the gardens this afternoon. Please go to the butcher and get me six ounces of liver and then to the greengrocer next door and buy just one orange."

Off we went joyful at pulling another fast one. It was about a ten minute walk to the high street and the butcher's shop was about half way down. We had been chatting away and praising our own ingenuity and as we approached the butchers Barry said...

"What did he ask us to get."

"A pound of liver and six oranges," I replied

So that's what he got, needless to say that was the last time he ever let us do his shopping for him, still I don't suppose he ever suffered from iron deficiency.

Chapter Three: Adolescence

From the living room came the sound of heavy footsteps...

I was now into my teenage years with all the challenges they bring not only for me but for my poor mother as well. Spots arrived - along with other things. Voice dropped - along with other things, and I was becoming a typical teenage brat. When away from home the F and C words became the main conjunctions in my sentences and, whenever my dad wasn't around, I was rude and verbally abusive to my mum. Cleanliness was not of great concern to me either and I would often wear the same socks for four days, until they stank along with my feet, or go to school with my trousers covering legs still splattered in mud from the football game the previous evening. Attending a single-sex school was limiting my personality. I was fine talking, swearing and interacting with boys, but if girls were bought into the group I would feel uncomfortable, blush and have no idea of what to say to them. It was a similar scenario to the Boxing Day family parties.

David and Peter were working men now, never home before five - thirty and Dad rarely before six. Often, we wouldn't see him until nine or ten, so Les and me were almost always the first home each weekday. It had reached a point when you could tell what dinner was going to be waiting for you when you got home from school. Monday egg and chips, Tuesday liver and mash, Thursday always fish and chips from the local chippie..., loved Thursdays, hated Tuesdays. I remember coming home one Tuesday...

"What's for dinner, Mum?"

"Liver and mash;" came the expected reply.

"I bloody hate liver, how many times do you have to be told, stupid woman;" I ranted.

From the living room came the sound of heavy footsteps and my father emerged, his face screwed up in rage. He had come home from work early and before I knew what was happening, he pulled me to him, sat on the stairs, put me across his knee and I felt the full force of his large hand on my backside as he hit me almost in unison to his words...

"Don't - you - ever - talk - to - your - mother - like - that - again - or - I'll - knock - your - bloody - block - off. You don't want your dinner so it's going in the bin. Now get up to your room and stay there!"

The following few days were very frosty although I did apologise to mum the next day.

I was still in bed by nine each evening, and if I wanted to go anywhere with my friends, I always had to ask first and be back in time for bed. All of my friends were allowed out till much later, so it reached the point where I would just say I couldn't go and make up any excuse to avoid being made to feel mollycoddled. One incident that gave me some incite as to why my parents were so restrictive, was when I asked if I could meet my friends at six o'clock to go to the large playing fields, about half a mile away, to play football. Dad said yes as long as I was back by nine. I was waiting for my friends about 300 yards away from the house when a man walked up to me and told me he was a detective investigating some burglaries in the area.

"Do you know who's been doing these break-ins?" he asked.

"No," I replied feeling very uncomfortable and a little scared.

"Who do you think might be responsible?"

Terrified, I named all the older boys in the area and pointed to where they lived. After he thanked me and went on his way, I ran straight home, shaking. Dad asked me what was wrong and when I told him he was fuming. He marched straight down to the Police Station and demanded to see the detective who had questioned a 13 year - old boy without any form of identification and without any parent present. The man really was a detective and was very apologetic, but he certainly knew he had done wrong by the time Dad had finished.

At home things carried on the same, Dad's moods, church on Sundays and, for me, Tuesday and Friday evenings when I went to Boy's Brigade at the local Baptist church. I joined because my brother Peter was involved and they played lots of sports. The church part of it didn't really appeal as throughout the many years of being made to go to Sunday school I had seen so much hypocrisy that it held very little meaning for me. I would see people acting righteous and kind on Sunday and then totally different away from church, and despite all my ranting teenage behaviour I always had my father's basic honesty and feeling for justice. But I also had a strong sense that a god source did exist.

In July 1969 I hit my 15th birthday and that September, started my fifth year at senior school. In those days you didn't have to stay on, so many of my classmates left school and went out into the world of work before any exams were taken, leaving about 12 pupils in the class. As a fifth-year you automatically became a Prefect which gave you a considerable amount of power over the younger pupils. The relationship with some of the teachers also changed. No longer Moore or Eames, you became Derek or Barry. I suppose that was their way of respecting you and treating you as an adult, although it would be fair to say many of us were years away from deserving that. It was fast approaching exam time and also the time when I needed to decide what I was going to do for a living. Earlier that year we had performed one of our plays at the local Drama College, after which a classmate and I were told that if we applied to the college we would almost certainly be accepted. I really fancied trying my hand at acting so I told my parents. My father just grimaced, said he couldn't afford to support me through four years of Drama school, and anyway it wasn't a proper job, I should get an apprenticeship like my brothers before me. So that was the end of that dream, but to be fair he really couldn't afford it and was already working long hours to support his family.

In the January of the following year I took the entrance exam for apprenticeships in Portsmouth Naval Dockyard and came 13th out of 299 which basically meant I had the choice of any apprenticeship I wanted. In February I went with Dad to the interview and chose to take an Electrical Fitters apprenticeship, including working with armaments, which meant that after two and a half years of my four year apprenticeship I would move to Gosport and learn to repair and test missiles and torpedoes. My father words ringing in my ears…

"They will always need electricians and electrical engineers."

I was to start work in May of 1970, two months before my 16th birthday, and at the interview I asked if there was any point in taking my exams and whether time off would be given to do so. I was told there was no need as I had already secured my future. At school the following day, I told them I was leaving to take up the offer of the apprenticeship and most seemed happy for me, but my English teacher was disappointed I would not be sitting the exam. He stopped the class, took me to one side, and enquired whether this was really what I wanted. I assured him it was, but in all honesty I don't think I had any clue what I wanted.

Chapter Four: Beginning Adulthood

I lifted my steel capped boot (we all had to wear these) and gently eased him over the toolbox...

The beginning of adulthood is a bit subjective, as where adolescence ends and adulthood begins is different for each individual. This was the time when my father started to treat me as an adult, although I don't believe I reached maturity until at least ten years later.

It was the first Sunday in May 1970 and I was to start my apprenticeship the following day. We had all eaten dinner and I had gone to my bedroom to dress in my Sunday best' as usual. I descended the stairs to find my father standing at the bottom in the hallway...

"What are you doing?" he asked.

"Getting ready for church," I replied.

"You start work tomorrow so now decisions are yours. You go if you want to but you no longer have to if you don't want to."

Without another word he then walked off into the front room. I couldn't get back upstairs quick enough to remove the restrictive clothing, and apart from weddings and funerals it was 17 years before I set foot in a church again. As far as Dad was concerned he had brought me up the best he could and now the reigns were off. I say off, but there were still house rules and an 11 o'clock curfew. I would be bringing home five pounds a week in the first year of work, with one third of this paid to my mother, the same proportion as paid into the household by both my brothers. I also now had to make my own bed and iron my own work shirts.

I arose on the Monday morning to be greeted by a hearty breakfast of bacon, eggs, tomatoes and toast all lovingly prepared by Mum, took the bus to the apprentice training centre called Flathouse (I believe it was named after the quayside it sat on) and was in my workshop promptly by

7.30am. One of about 13 or 14 lads, plus two girls as this was the first year of female intakes, I seemed to be the only person who knew no-one at all and felt a little out of place. Our two instructors introduced themselves and gave us a briefing on what was expected in terms of behaviour, set us up on workstations and promptly gave us our first task - which was to take up the first two weeks of my working life - to file a perfect two inch cube of brass into a perfect one inch cube! We were told there would also be written theory tests and a three month review when, anyone thought not able to use their tools correctly or did not score at least 50% in the theory, would politely be asked to leave. Copies of reviews, along with comments, would be sent to parents. At this point alarm bells started ringing, as any practical work was going to be a real struggle. My dad, god bless him would turn his hands to any task at home, be it decorating, gardening or repairing dripping taps, and he had always tried to get us involved, show us how things were done. He wasn't the best but most of his work was passable. I, being a lazy child couldn't and didn't want to learn and would try as hard as I could to get out of anything that involved hard work.

There we all were filing away, most chatting to each other across the workbenches and me feeling isolated and detached. We were allowed two 15 minute breaks, one morning, one afternoon and an hour for lunch. On the second morning break everyone was standing around talking and I was thinking: "I can't spend the next four years not saying anything," when the boy next to me bent down to put something into his toolbox. I lifted my steel capped boot (we all had to wear these) and gently eased him over the toolbox onto the floor. Everybody laughed and he turned round and asked...

"What did you do that for?"

"Because I don't know anyone" I replied holding my hand out to help him back to his feet.

"You could have just bloody spoken to me" he said laughing himself now. "I'm John."

"I'm Derek, nice to meet you John."

I held out my hand again and he shook it and then everyone else began to introduce themselves to me, but John was to be my best mate during those first two years.

When I handed my one inch not so perfect cube over to the instructors two weeks later, they applied a set square to it and you could have driven a bus through the gaps on every side, but they made no comment, just labelled it with my name. The next task was to make a steel 'G'-clamp which stayed in your toolbox for the rest of your working life.

We had a variety of personalities in our group. The two girls were from Southampton, renting rooms during the week and going home at weekends. Then there was Bill who, along with me, was still 15 when we started; everyone else was 16. Although the youngest, everybody seemed to know Bill was the strongest and, at six feet plus, not to be argued with. He nicknamed me Tom as he didn't like Derek and I always got on well with him. If I was short of money he would walk me round to his house and get me the bus fare home.

George and his mate rode motorbikes and would come into work in all their leathers. George rode a 650cc Triumph Bonneville and as he lived within a half mile of me would sometimes give me a lift home which I found both frightening and exhilarating at the same time. During the first six weeks people would go missing for a couple of days and I found out later that they were off doing exams and I ended up being the only one that hadn't bothered.

During break times things were getting a bit more boisterous and one particular day George decided to fill someone's bicycle pump with water and squirt it at everyone in sight. I was talking to John as George approached a lad called Rod, whom John had gone to school with, waving the pump...

"Don't you fucking come near me with that," Rod warned.

John and I stopped our conversation and looked on.

"Don't do it George," Rod said again.

John turned to me and said: "Look at Rod's hand behind his back. He's going to crack him if he doesn't walk away."

George was almost twice the size of Rod but that didn't seem to matter because as George fired the water Rod's fist hit him hard in the face and blood started to flow from his nose and mouth. All hell broke loose, George picked up a scriber (a thin sharp tool used to mark out measurements on metal) and the chase began, Rod running around the workbenches laughing, George pursuing in tears trying to stab him. The two instructors came rushing down from the far end of the workshop and it took both of them to restrain George. The two lads were taken away and only George returned. I never saw Rod again.

John and I were becoming good mates and we both tried out successfully for the Portsmouth dockyard table tennis team. We played matches in the local league on Tuesday evenings at the apprentices club in Conway Street, where the second year of our training would take place, or at the home venues of the other teams. Teams consisted of four players and matches were four singles and one doubles, so when one of our elder players no longer wanted to play, we were guaranteed a game every match. One Tuesday evening we found out what a small world it was. We went for tea with John's aunt and uncle as they lived only a half mile from the club. On the first visit John's aunt remarked that she had seen Ben Moore that day.

"Do you mean Ben Moore who lives in Waterlooville and is a volunteer fireman?" I enquired.

"Yes."

"That's my uncle," I said.

"His wife Enid is my niece," she replied.

So the person I had chosen to kick over his toolbox is related to me in some way or other, but please don't ask me to work out how.

I now had two groups of friends, those from my work and

those from home, two entirely separate parts of my life. Apart from John I hardly saw any of my workmates in the evenings except for the odd occasion when I would go to the apprentice's club. I found it easier to stay around my home area due to the 11 o'clock curfew. I felt my work friends would not understand that I had to be home at a certain time as they appeared to have far more freedom. At 16 my evenings were spent playing football or going in a group to the cinema and trying to get into the 18 and over features. In those days they were categorised as X films.

When the three month review arrived, the first I knew of it was when I arrived home one evening to a very vocal and disappointed father who let me have it with both barrels.

"What the bloody hell is this all about?" he raged, waving what was obviously my report. "12% for your first piece of work" (the filing exercise)" 23% for the second," ('G'-clamp). This says they are only letting you continue because your theory was 95%. You'd better pull your bloody finger out, this is your future. I don't want to see another report like this again."

I never said a word in my defence, just went away to sulk thinking: "...not my fault if I'm no bloody good at metalwork."

I don't know if any further reports were sent but if they were I must have improved because he never mentioned anything again.

During the four years of the apprenticeship one day a week would be spent at college studying for an ONC in Electrical Engineering, ONC standing for Ordinary National Certificate. From that, you could go on to study for your HNC or Higher National Certificate.

For the second year of training we moved to the Conway Street centre and this was much more to my liking as here we would learn to use a lathe. At last a machine that took away all the guess work and actually produced what was needed without all the filing and hard work. Right up my street. We would also learn how to wire up electrical circuits and repair motors, alternators and various pieces of electrical equipment. This year at work passed with no major catastrophes, in fact the most difficult thing for me was avoiding the drugs which were widely used by my colleagues. We had one lad injecting himself with heroin and I had suspicions of another. During lunch breaks a couple of lads would sniff boot polish, sometimes pass out and it would take a bottle of water poured over them to bring them round, but mainly LSD tablets were the problem. If you didn't keep tight hold on your jam doughnuts a tablet would be shoved into the jam hole and we had a couple of occasions when those not interested in drugs suddenly found themselves flying with Lucy. I was very careful, managed to avoid any such occurrences and have to say that I never felt the slightest inclination to take drugs other than the usual teenager's need for alcohol, although I did smoke from the age of 16 to 29. When my father saw me with my first cigarette he just said...

"Oh well son, someday you'll regret it."

He was right. Both he and my mother were smokers although Dad did manage to quit, but even after 30 years he would say that any time he felt stressed he would find his hand reaching out for the packet. Mum smoked throughout her adult life and was rarely without a fag on the go, but the surprising thing was that when she was nearly 80 years of age she told me that she had never inhaled. During lunch breaks at work John and I would often go for a pint and a pie at a small corner street pub we had found. The landlady knew we were under age but told us she would only serve us with one pint each and didn't want to see us at any time other than weekday lunchtimes.

At the beginning of the third year we all entered the actual dockyard, were split up and placed with qualified fitters and their labourers or fitter's mates as they were known. My first three month placement was in the submarine section and then I moved on to frigates and destroyers for the next three months. I am embarrassed to say that my work was never of the highest quality, everything was wired correctly but it was never neat and my mentor would always have to tidy it up.

At the end of the six-months I was due to be placed in the armaments depots in Gosport.

It was not long before this move that I had my first bad experience with alcohol. Malcolm, a friend who lived in a third storey flat nearby home invited me to his sister's wedding party held at the Labour club in Cosham. All drinks were free and there was a big buffet of amazing food, which I never got to sample because Malcolm and I decided that we would have a drinking contest. This started with a couple of pints chased down with whiskies, followed by rum and blacks, many of which were doubles. I think at the last count I had had 15, but to be truthful it could have been a lot more. When I got home and lay in my bed the whole room was spinning and I was lying in masses of purple vomit. I don't know if I slept at all that night, but at about seven in the morning I looked at the state of the bed and thought; "My god he's going to kill me." I went downstairs to wash myself down, feeling so ill, suddenly the thought that if I took the dog out for an hour it would save Dad from having to do it after breakfast and put him in a good mood. I trundled to the playing fields with Lady, our beautiful Heinz (fifty seven varieties) mongrel, dreading the thought of telling Mum and Dad, and for that matter not feeling like eating a massive fried Sunday breakfast when I got home.

As the dog and I walked in the door Dad was just dishing up…

"Where have you been?" he asked.

"I was up early so thought I would take Lady for her walk."

"Oh, thanks very much."

I thought: "First part of the plan successful," as he had a smile on his face.

How I managed to eat the breakfast without being sick I shall never know, but then I had to pluck up courage to speak.

"I've got something I need to tell you."

"Oh yes, what's that then?"

I remember my exact words: "I had one over the eight last night and I've been a bit sick over the bed."

"So" brief pause… "What time did you get home last night?"

"Well I remember seeing Malcolm to his front door at about a quarter to 11 so about five minutes after that."

I actually remembered pushing him up the two flights stairs to his of flat and shoving him head first through the door, which I believe was open at the time.

"You rolled in here at three o'clock this morning and made more noise trying to be quiet, shushing and giggling. Now how bad is the mess upstairs?"

"It's pretty bad."

He then looked me in the eye and in a quiet voice said:

"Ok, when you've finished breakfast you will go and strip your bed. The Launderette is open this morning so you will take your bedding and pay to wash and dry it, your mother is not doing it for you." He then smiled at me and whispered: "You look ill Son, won't be doing that again will you?"

"No Dad."

I still to this day don't know what happened in that four hours between Malcolm's flat and home, the only two things I do remember are walking down the middle of the Western road (the same road I had been run over on), and bumping into a lamp post.

Chapter Five: The Gosport Years

"Nobody will sign any forms for you unless you break your fucking neck...

On completing the first two and a half years of my apprenticeship I was transferred to Elson in Gosport. Elson and Frater, the two depots where I would finish my apprenticeship and work for the next five years, were separated by a half- mile long internal road. The previous week I had received a letter at home, luckily addressed to me and not my father, telling me that I was no longer welcome to attend the college course at Highbury Technical College. I had passed my two-year exams but this was the result of a sarcastic answer to a lecturer who took the last lesson of each college day. This lecturer had a high pitched voice that would send me to sleep, that's my excuse and I'm sticking to it, and on this particular day he had seen me dosing off and shouted across the classroom...

"What was the last thing I said Moore?"

I replied: "What was the last thing I said Moore?"

The class laughed.

"You get on my fucking tits."

No more was said, the lesson continued and I thought that was the end of the matter but he had obviously taken it further. The most surprising thing was that in moving to Gosport the following Monday I heard no more about it and nobody questioned why I wasn't going on day-release to college each Tuesday. If I had still been in Portsmouth Dockyard it would have undoubtedly been picked-up and I would probably have been out of a job.

On my first day in Elson I was taken to a room and told to sit down and read a manual and this I did -for the next three months - the same bloody manual. Nobody interacted with me I was just left on my own. I got so bored that I started taking what was left of my yearly paid leave in afternoons-off and when the paid leave was gone, I took unpaid. These afternoons I would spend either at the cinema or in the bookmakers, making sure I arrived home at my usual time. At the end of three months I was put with a group working on Electronic Torpedoes. At this point I have to be careful, I had to sign the official secrets act so I don't think I am permitted to go into any great detail of the work involved. Although at this point, I was still not allowed to touch anything, so when the two weeks permitted unpaid leave was finished I just went off in the afternoons anyway.

After six months in Elson I was sent up the road to Frater and after a brief spell working on large batteries I was transferred to the Mechanical Torpedo factory where I would survive the next three and a half years, but only just.

I was now in a rut and continuing to find ways of getting out of the whole horrible environment. I don't mean the people I worked with, most of whom were good hard working men and I had some great times with my workmates, but I definitely knew that I was not cut out to be an electrical fitter. I was only surviving due to the fact that each procedure was written down, and as long as you followed the instructions the job would get done. I suppose I had been in the torpedo factory about eight months when the door to the foreman's office opened and a booming voice was heard…

"Derek Moore, get your arse in here now."

I had never been in the foreman's office before and just knew his name was Harry. As I walked in I could see he had a stern look on his face.

"Don't sit down, just stand there," he commanded. "Now let's look at your record, you've had three weeks paid leave which you're entitled to, two weeks unpaid leave which you're entitled to and 20 days casual sick of which you are only entitled to ten, but we have paid you for all of them. Not your fault, our mistake. Migraine, gastro enteritis, diarrhoea and ailments that I have never even heard of, how you're still alive I have no idea. On top of all this we have 114 hours absent time. What bloody excuse do you have?"

"None"

Some of the lads were now peering through the office window and laughing.

"Go away you morons," he shouted.

"None, well at least you're not making up feeble excuses like these bloody ailments. Let's get something straight, I don't care if you go out of the gate right now, but I'm telling you that nobody will sign any forms for you unless you break your fucking neck, now get out of my office."

I was to spend the next five months without a day off, but it wasn't over yet. I was about three weeks from completing my training when a letter arrived inviting me to a formal interview with the top man dealing with apprentices in the dockyard, to discuss my disciplinary record. I could take a union representative with me and in fact the letter advised me to do so. The interview was a couple of days later at about 11 in the morning.

"So Mr Moore, I'm looking at this review of your training as I do with all apprentices before their indentures are issued and they become fully qualified, and I can see that when you entered Elson a pattern of absenteeism began. Can you explain this to me?"

My union rep and I had pre-empted this so I had my answer ready.

"Well, you sent me over there and told me to sit down and read a book for three months, with nobody taking any interest in me I got bored to tears, so at lunchtimes I would just leave sir."

I don't remember the exact conversation, but he looked surprised by this answer and the outcome was that he ended up apologising to me, and told me my indentures would be signed and sent to me by the end of the week, when I Derek Moore would be a fully qualified electrical fitter. Not only this, he then asked which side of the water I lived on and when I said Portsmouth, he said it was unfair to bring me over and then send me back, costing me double bus fares, so I might as well go home. So I got another afternoon off.

How the hell did that happen?

My indentures arrived as promised and I was feeling chuffed. Wages rose considerably to about thirty pounds a week which could be further increased by productivity bonus, and I would be in charge of a labourer who I could get to do all the crappy jobs. During my first day as a qualified fitter the charge-hand Alan told me to report to the foreman immediately. I went to his office and he beckoned me in and told me to sit down.

"The first thing I want to do is congratulate you on completing your apprenticeship; it just goes to show that miracles do happen."

"Thanks Harry."

"Don't thank me because the second thing I want to do is wring your bloody neck. I have just had Portsmouth on the phone and they have given me the biggest bollocking I've had in thirty years. When I asked you if you had any excuse for you absenteeism you categorically said no, but now I hear it's entirely our fault and you are not to blame at all."

"I had to have something to tell them Harry and it was the truth."

He just glared at me and told me to go. I walked out of the office and went back to work.

That evening I had arranged to meet the lads in a pub in Gosport called The Dolphin to celebrate my rise to prominence. As I walked into the pub I saw Harry at the bar looking at me and beckoning me over.

"What do you want to drink lad?"

"Pint of bitter please" I replied, totally bewildered. "This morning you were giving me a bollocking and now you're the first person to buy me a drink, I don't understand."

"Outside of work you are a really likeable lad, inside work you are a pain in the arse. We're outside now so drink up, let's get sloshed."

I gained real respect for Harry that evening and believe me when I say we did get blathered.

In the next few months I took on the role as a union representative, not because I had any great knowledge of industrial rules and regulations, but because it would make me almost impossible to sack.

Harry wasn't the only authority figure I was to have problems with. Our charge-hand and I developed a real dislike for each other. It started when I politely declined his request to do overtime on a particular job and he moved on to ask others. A friend Al asked why I didn't want the overtime.

"Because I leave here at four thirty, it takes me an hour and a half to get home and by the time I've had dinner it's gone seven and I play darts at seven thirty."

"Look" he said, "You work here till six, I'll give you a lift home as you're only five minutes out of my way and you'll still be in the pub for your darts match."

I shouted across the shop floor: "Hey Alan, I will do overtime."

He shouted back: "Too bloody late now." In reply to which I shouted: "Stuff your overtime up your fucking arse then."

He came storming over to me...

"You can't swear at me, I'll have you up on a charge."

"Have me up on a charge you jumped up tosser, where are all your witnesses?"

As he looked around all the lads turned away and got on with their work. From that moment I considered him an arsehole and he thought I was an ignorant brat. I think we might agree now that we were both probably correct to a point. The next three years passed without any significant changes, although I still took most of my leave in half days just to get out of the place. The lads nicknamed me 'Leave Chit Moore,' and there were not many times when I worked a full week during the year. In 1976 Alan got an opportunity to get me out of his section and place me in a soul destroying workshop where most days you were filing rust off of equipment to try to bring it back to a useable state. This transfer was to signal the beginning of the end for this job and line of work.

I am not sure I have placed this at the right time in my story but I won't be far out. My gran had been ill for some time and sadly passed away at 89 years of age. Standing by the grave side I noticed a distinct coldness between members of the family, there had obviously been a falling out which had split them into two distinct groups. I had never been told what the problem was and when we left the funeral I decided that I wasn't going to ask, that as far as I was concerned everyone was my family and I would still treat them as such. This disagreement did bring a stop to the Boxing Day parties and went on for many years, although I am glad to say that before any of them passed it was resolved and brothers and sisters were all close again.

At home my dad was beginning to see how unhappy I was and in May 1977 he came home from work with an application form for me.

"I have a vacancy for a technical clerk in my office, so if you want an interview complete the form and I will take it into Personnel for you."

I looked at the form and found that I would have to drop about nine pounds a week, but as I was paying that out on bus fares my financial position was not going to change, so I filled in the form and Dad took it in the following morning. Within two weeks I had a date for an interview in my dad's office. He had told two of his senior estimators, Pat and Syd, to conduct my interview and it would be their decision as to whether I would be offered the position. This was typical of my father's honesty. Two weeks later I received a letter offering me the job with a starting date of July fourth, my birthday. In that two week period my dad was promoted to chief estimator of the Marconi group and although he would work in the same factory as me he was not going to be my immediate boss. This may have been a blessing in disguise. He also received a letter saying he was being awarded an MBE for services to exports.

I went into Frater the next morning and with tremendous relief handed in my notice. On the day of my leaving Harry, came to say goodbye and said…

"If you ever want to come back give me a ring."

Pretty sure he didn't mean it.

Chapter Six: A New Start

"Is this your first day here shit face"...

My first day at Marconi's and I arrived to find that Syd, one of the two men that had interviewed me, was now chief estimator and Pat, the other interviewer, was to be my section leader. I could not have been placed on a better section as Pat was a straight talking but very loyal man. There were four sections in the department each consisting of a section leader, two senior estimators and two technical clerks. The other two estimators on my section were Arthur and an Irishman called Ken both of whom were again straight talking honest men and a privilege to know and work with. I was placed with the other technical clerk Steve, who was training to be an estimator, and he took me around the office to introduce me to everyone. One man, called Eddie, just grunted at me when I was introduced and then made his way into Syd's office where he apparently asked if I was Arthur Moore's son and was that the reason I had been given the job. I was to have a few disputes with Syd over the coming ten years, but on this occasion he sent Eddie from his office with a flea in his ear, telling him that he had interviewed me along with Pat and they had the say as to whether I was given the Job. As he left the office I smiled sweetly at him and was tempted to blow him a kiss. Pat saw this and just smiled a smile that said; "You'll do." I was later to learn that Pat had been a spitfire pilot during the war, although the only snippets you would get from him about this time were when he'd had a few to drink, and even then he wasn't very forthcoming. When I had been introduced to everyone, Steve who was about three years older than me said...

"You won't remember me but we have met before. You used to live next door to me in Paulsgrove and my mum's chickens pecked your fingers."

Small world again!

Steve then passed me on to another section's clerk Ron, who was also the Shop Steward, and his job was to teach me how to put items lists into order ready for scheduling. I won't go into boring detail, but having shown me once he produced a large pile of lists and told me to put them in order. A simple task really, that took me about five minutes. He then checked them and remarked...

"They're ok. Now I'm going to throw them on the floor so that they are all out of order and you have to put them back again."

As he began to pick them up from the desk I quietly and politely said...

"If you throw them on the floor Ron, you'll be picking them up. If you want to mix them up again and get me to sort them then that's fine, but don't take me for a fool because I'm quite capable of standing up for myself."

Normally I wouldn't have been that polite but it was my first day and I didn't really want to be making enemies.

Pat just turned his head and with that same smile said...

"You've done enough of that crap, come back to your seat and we'll get you working."

I went home that evening thinking this is more like it, I can enjoy this and I think I'm going to be good at it.

Every Friday dinnertime Pat would have us over the bar till about two o'clock. He never asked what you wanted to drink he would just order five pints of bitter. The other section leaders, one of whom was my uncle Sid (married to my dad's sister Joyce and not to be confused with Syd) were not happy that we had a two hour lunch-break on a Friday but Pat couldn't care less and it would be fair to say we produced as much, if not more, quality work on our section as they did. We were pricing up Ministry contracts worth millions of pounds and I found I had an ability to look at a column of figures and the total at the bottom of the page and just know if there was a mistake.

On the side, I had also started to work in a pub called The

Wymering Arms which was a short walk from home. I would work two evenings a week and Sunday lunch time for a total of ten pounds which, to be honest, I had usually spent drinking behind the bar when I was working or after last orders. After the pub closed and everything was cleared and washed, Charlie the landlord would take all the staff into the lounge bar and we would drink till three in the morning. No money would go into the till but it would be left by the side, to be rung up the next morning just after opening time. This job really has no relevance to my story although I must say that for the three years I worked there I really enjoyed it. I have mentioned it because of two humorous incidents. My first evening working, a man came into the bar with a large Alsatian dog. I asked him what he would like and he just stared at me and then asked...

"Is this your first day here shit face?"

"Yes," I replied feeling quite intimidated. He was a man in his late twenties and built, as we say, like a brick shithouse.

"Brown Split wanker"

I poured his pint and placed it on the bar in front of him...

"Thanks bastard"

This abuse went on all evening. When we were in the lounge bar after work Charlie asked...

"How did your first evening go?"

"Fine thanks Charlie, except for the big bastard with the Alsatian who just kept abusing me all night."

"Oh, that's Colin; just give him back what he dishes out."

"Have you seen the size of him?"

"Don't worry about that, just stick up for yourself."

It's my next evening at work and in walks Colin and his beautifully behaved dog.

"Brown Split shit face."

Plucking up every ounce of courage I replied...

"One Brown Split coming up arsehole."

His face changed into a menacing stare as I poured and placed his pint in front of him.

"Thanks tosser."

"You're welcome pig face."

He stood up, leaned across the bar and with one hand grasping my collar he lifted me off my feet so that my face was no more than an inch from his and I thought my days were numbered; and then his eyes lit up and with a broad grin he whispered...

"Charlie's had a word with you hasn't he?"

From that moment, we got on like a house on fire and I was to later play football in the same team as him.

Sometime later, the first person to come in during an evening shift was an old school friend I hadn't seen for many years. Dave had been a brilliant footballer, who as a junior had played for the senior team. We had all expected him to go on to play professionally, but unfortunately drink and drugs had taken priority in his life. He sat at the bar all evening and as we reminisced about school days he was getting more and more intoxicated. When last orders were called and everyone started to drink up and leave Dave remained still sat on his stool at the bar.

"Come on Dave, time to go home" said Charlie.

"I wanna fight you Charlie" said Dave.

"Don't be stupid Dave, go on home."

"Not until we've had a fight."

This went on for five or so minutes then Charlie asked...

"You really want a fight Dave?"

"Yeah"

"Well just hang on there a minute and I'll come round to that side of the bar".

With that Charlie disappeared through to the adjoining corridor and Dave and I waited for him to reappear in the bar.

A few minutes later Charlie re-appeared but again on my side of the bar.

"You sure you want a fight Dave?"

"Yeah Charlie you coward, get your arse round here."

"Are you absolutely sure you want to fight?"

Before Dave could answer the main doors to the pub opened and in walked two policemen and Charlie said...

"Fight them then you bastard."

As the two policemen dragged Dave from the pub he added...

"By the way, you're barred."

I never saw Dave in the pub again although I did hear that he had gone in to apologise.

My love life was still nothing to write home about due to my continued shyness around the opposite sex. I had had a one night stand and a slightly longer relationship with a married barmaid who worked at the pub, all of these instigated by the girls. After that there was a relationship with a girl called Jenny who had worked in the offices at Frater. She and her husband had had twin girls and had broken-up when the girls were about a year old. We started going out together and this was my first real love, but it ended after about 18 months when she told me she couldn't be with me anymore. I was very hurt and very bitter and said some awful things to her. About six months later she re-married to a man named Bill who had also worked at Frater and had been my labourer for a while. I must say he was a great fun guy to be around. Jenny's mother and I had always got on well, and after the breakup we would still keep in touch by sending each other Christmas cards, in which she would keep me up to date with all that was happening in her family, including that Jenny and Bill had a daughter Lucy.

At Marconi things were going well and I had made friends with two lads, Martin and Paul, who had joined about six months after I had. Martin had converted us to golf and we would play most weekends and during the summer months when the evenings were light, after work. Both lads were married although Paul was to lose his wife in the early eighties to cancer, but within a couple of years he would re-marry and go on to have two boys. Martin also had two children, one boy and one girl. When we were not playing golf we would be in the snooker hall or at Martin's house where his front room was a little like a pub, fixed up with a small snooker table and a dartboard. I would quite often babysit for him and his wife, sleep on the sofa and then we would be at the golf course by seven the following morning. In the following years Martin and I would hire a caravan from a man who worked in a different department at Marconi and have a seven days holiday playing golf in Devon.

After three years I left the pub because promotion at work meant that I couldn't promise to be free on those evenings any more. I say promotion but that's not strictly true. Steve had been offered an estimators job with another company and decided to take up the offer, so Syd had then offered me Steve's place on the estimators' training course with the promise that if he got satisfactory reports from all of the different department heads that I would be spending time with, I would go straight to estimator grade and the appropriate wage rise would follow. The course also demanded that I had to go to night school and achieve 'O' level English and Maths, so with that and the evening golf there was no room for working in the pub.

The estimators' training course normally lasted two years, but I was told that because I could already read Mechanical and Electrical drawings the course would be only one year for me. The maths course, at the same technical college I had been thrown out of some ten years earlier, only lasted three weeks. On week one there were over twenty students, by week two this was down to about twelve and week three only three of us turned up so they cancelled the course. When I told Syd he just said he had seen enough of my maths to know I was more than capable so not to worry about it.

More changes on the home front as Dad was fast approaching retirement and his new position seemed to have mellowed him. The dark moods were now few and far between and he spent much of his working weeks in Hillend, Scotland or Kidsgrove, which I believe is near Manchester. When he was in Portsmouth he would be tucked away in his office talking to ministry people and trying to negotiate the best price for the company. I would often spend ten minutes or so chatting to his secretary Mary who was to be of great assistance to me in my later ventures and become a great friend. My brother David had decided to leave the dockyard and join the army, signing on for a full twenty two year stint. He had had his own relationship breakdown which had hurt him, but whilst stationed in Edinburgh he was to meet Lynn, an army nurse and they would go on to marry and have three children, Andrew and twin girls Wendy and Victoria. My sister, Lesley, had left school and was working for Midland Bank (now HSBC) and had met a grand chap Andy who she married in 1981. My other brother Peter, Dad and I decided to buy the house in Cosham over a five year period, so that Mum and Dad would have their own property by the time he retired. This meant that I was committed to staying at least until the mortgage was paid off. Peter and I then had an arrangement whereby he would buy my quarter of the house and I would have the deposit for a place of my own. All of this was only possible because of the buy your council house scheme brought in by Margaret Thatcher in the late seventies. Cousin Chrissie had run off to Gretna Green and married at a very young age, had two children, got divorced and remarried, had two more children, and I had lost track of her, but she was to re-emerge in my life many years later.

I obtained my English qualification and was called into Syd's office at the end of my training period...

"I'm very pleased with the reports I have in front of me Derek and can say you have passed the course with flying colours."

I thought to myself, big pay rise coming now.

"From Monday you will be on grade seven and begin as a fully-fledged estimator."

"Grade seven Syd," I queried because an estimators starting salary was at grade eight.

"Yes," he said.

"But you promised me that if I met all of your criteria I would be put on an estimator's salary."

"I can't justify that sort of raise so I've invented an interim grade for one year."

I was now getting angry and was about to revert back to old ways.

"But you promised."

"I can't bloody do it."

"So what you're saying Syd is that your word isn't worth a fucking toss."

I just couldn't believe his reply to this...

"That's right."

I looked at him, scowled and as I got up to leave the office said...

"There's no fucking answer to that, is there?"

I apologised for the language to his secretary Sandra as I passed her desk. She smiled and whispered...

"That's ok, I don't blame you."

At this time our original section had been split-up because we had moved offices and I was now working for Ken who had been promoted to section leader. We still went to the bar each Friday with Pat's section so there was no change there.

The day after my spat with Syd, he called Ken into his office to tell him that the job we were working on was becoming urgent, so he was authorising overtime for the following two weeks so the job could be finished. This meant working evenings and weekends. Ken came out to tell us this was what was expected and I told him that I wasn't available for overtime.

"Why not?" he asked.

"Because as far as I'm concerned the more hours I work the more money I'm losing by not being on the right grade," I replied.

He turned and walked back into the office to tell Syd, and although he didn't call me in or come out to see me everyone in the office heard his anger.

Across the office Pat smiled, and I went home at four thirty.

The next morning I was summoned to Syd's office.

"You're on grade eight; I've had to stick my neck out to get this for you. Now will you do overtime?"

He looked at me as if I should be grateful, but if he thought I was going to thank him he would be waiting a long time.

"Yes," I replied and stood up to leave. As I reached the door he said...

"When you see Mrs Welch make sure you say thank you to her."

She was the managing director's secretary who had been Syd's secretary when I first joined the company and I had always got on well with her. She had a wicked sense of humour and a laugh to match and I was always telling her jokes, most of which would be considered non PC these days.

"Why?"

Doesn't matter why, just say it."

That dinner hour I went over to the sub-branch of the Midland bank we had inside the work's perimeter and Mrs Welch was in the queue so I leaned across and said...

"Thank you."

"What for?" she asked.

"Haven't got a clue, Syd just told me that I was to thank you when I saw you."

"Oh, that's because when my boss saw the request for your grading rise he asked me if you were Arthur Moore's son. When I said yes he threw it to one side and said he wasn't going to sign it, so I picked it up, put it back in front of him and told him to sign it as you'd had enough promises to you broken. So he signed it."

So Syd had had nothing to do with it. It was because of her that I was now grade eight.

Chapter Seven: A Racy Time

Plucking up all my courage I asked: "Would you like to go for a drink sometime"...

From quite an early age, I had an interest in horseracing. It had begun in 1964 when my brother Peter had put a one shilling bet on the Grand National for me. The horse's name was Team Spirit. I had been watching Saturday afternoon racing on Grandstand and World of Sport and become enthralled by this horse as he seemed so much smaller than those he raced against. Anyway, he won the race and that fuelled my interest so that when I started work I would go into the local bookmakers each Saturday and bet on the races that were to be televised. I would only bet in ten pence wagers and now and again Dad would go halves with me, although he would never sit and watch. He taught me that once a bet was placed the money was gone and if anything came back it was a bonus. I have always remembered those words and used them as my principle for gambling. Never put on what you are not willing to lose.

My local bookies was managed by a lady called Judy who I always got on with and there was always a bit of flirting between us, mostly instigated by little innuendos she would throw out at me based on the name of a horse I had backed that day. One morning at work a colleague on the shop floor stopped me and inquired...

"Do you know Judy in the R & G betting shop in Cosham?"

"Yes!"

"She's always talking about you and I reckon if you asked her out she'd say yes."

Well I couldn't stop thinking about this during the day, but having never really made the first move before I was in two minds whether or not to follow it up. That is a lie really because I wanted to ask her out, but didn't know if I had the courage to do so. On leaving work I made my way to the bookies and sat on one of the stools until the last race of the day had finished and all the punters had left. The lady who worked with Judy came into the front of the shop to sweep up all the losing betting slips that had been unceremoniously dumped on the floor.

"Come on Derek, home time."

I just sat there whilst she swept around me.

"Are you not going home tonight then?" she asked.

Judy saw me looking uncomfortable and said…

"Do you want to speak to me Derek?"

"Yes please," I replied.

She came out to me and we went outside. Plucking up all my courage I asked…

"Would you like to go for a drink sometime?"

"That's very kind but unfortunately I don't think my boyfriend would like it very much."

My heart fell into my stomach and I could feel myself blushing, and I was also thinking what a bastard the chap at work was for putting me in this position.

"I'm sorry I didn't realise, I hope you didn't mind me asking."

"Not at all, I'm actually pleased you did."

I went to work the next day and thanked the chap for making me look like a right Wally, not realising at the time that that was Judy's surname, Whalley. About a week later he came up to me and said that Judy wanted to see me and would I pop into the bookies that evening. When I got there she told me that she had split from her boyfriend and was free to go for a drink if the offer was still open. This was the beginning of a relationship which was to last about eight months.

Sometime prior to this, a work colleague Rick had decided to set up a little racing club. He would collect money from people each week and organise trips to a couple of race meetings each year. We had been to Lingfield Park, Ascot,

Sandown Park and to watch The Oaks at Epsom. He had decided that because of the success of those trips it would be good fun to take everyone abroad, so he had organised a weekend trip to Ostend where we would go racing on the Saturday afternoon, have the evening in Ostend, go to Bruges the following morning and return home on the overnight ferry to Dover. We would all go on these trips, Martin and Paul with their wives, Hilda our new office secretary with her boyfriend Steve. Hilda was a great northern girl, I believe originally from Burnley and what you saw was what you got, honest, straight-forward with a great sense of humour. This was very close to the time when I met Judy so when one person dropped out I was able to secure her a place on the coach. Everybody enjoyed this trip so much and I got to know Judy and started to have deep feelings for her. Rick had decided that the trip the following year was going to be to see The Arc de Triomphe in France, so we all started saving for this from the moment the Ostend trip had finished. Judy was not to make this trip with me because before the time came and just when I was going to propose, her old boyfriend appeared back on the scene and, without going into too much detail, through emotional blackmail had convinced her to move away from Portsmouth and start afresh with him in London. When she told me I was surprised by my reaction which was very brief...

"I don't want you to go, but I'm not going to try to stop you as you have to make the choice."

She chose to go, but a week later I received a package with no letter, just a cassette of love songs inside. Judy was to re-enter my life, briefly, but I have to say that this break up did not affect me in the same way as the previous one. I just decided to get on with it and from day one just carried on as normal, so perhaps my feelings weren't that deep after all.

Our first trip to Longchamp near Paris was in 1984 when the race was won by the French horse Sagace. This trip went well, we all got drunk and had a really good time, but from a betting point of view it was not profitable and we learnt that betting in France was a bit of a pain as there were no on course bookmakers and all betting went through the Tote which was run by the French government. This meant that if you had a winner there was a long delay before you were paid out, so when the following year's trip came around I put most people's bets on in England before we went and I had talked most of them into backing a horse called Rainbow Quest ridden by Pat Eddery, my favourite jockey. Eddery had ridden the horse in six of its races and if my memory serves me right had never been beaten on him. As the coach arrived at the racecourse two elderly ladies asked one of the lads we knew as Boofy if he would place their bets for them as they didn't have a clue as to how to do it. They both wanted five pounds to win on Rainbow Quest and this Boofy agreed to do.

The race went off and coming into the final furlong it had developed into a match between Rainbow Quest and the previous year's winner Sagace. We all cheered and shouted but to no avail as Sagace won by a very narrow margin. As we made our way to the winners enclosures to see the horses come back in I noticed my mate Dave with Boofy, both of them were looking very pleased and I thought those two sods have had the winner. I had known Dave most of my life as he lived on the Isle of Wight estate quite close to me, and as kids we would arrange football matches between the kids on his estate and those of us from the avenues. He was a very good footballer and was usually on the winning side and I must also say he was a great guy as well. Dave had joined Marconi a few years after me and had come into our office as a clerk being placed on the same section as me. We would meet in the mornings and walk to work and return home together most days. I should clarify that this was not the same person as the Dave mentioned in the pub story.

Whilst we were watching the horses being unsaddled a musical tune played out over the tannoy and a voice said two words in French. I went over to a group of men all talking in English and asked…

"Excuse me do you know what's happening?"

"Eddery has objected to the winner and he's pretty sure he'll be awarded the race," one of the men replied.

After what seemed an age the result was overturned and Rainbow Quest was announced the winner. The French jockey had been seen to whip the face of our horse and so he was disqualified. We'd all won money and I would pick it up in England when we returned. It was going to be a good evening in France before we boarded the late night ferry back to Newhaven. When we left the course and boarded the coach Boofy was on the back seat looking mortified.

"What are you looking so glum about, were you on the French horse?" I enquired.

Boofy didn't answer, but Dave did…

"He's upset because he didn't think that Rainbow Quest had a snowballs chance in hell of winning so not only has he lost his bet on Sagace, but he pocketed the ten pounds that the two ladies gave him to place their bets, so now he's got to pay each of them 45 pounds out of his own pocket."

We nearly wet ourselves laughing, especially as Boofy was not known for opening his wallet without a great deal of persuasion.

The racing trips were to continue until Rick left the company in the late eighties, by which time we had been to Deauville races twice and visited a few other British courses.

Chapter Eight: Loneliness

"I don't let anybody really know me because if they did they wouldn't...

By the light of the fire you sit in your chair
Gaze at four walls in total despair
Another day over and home by yourself
Get up from the chair, tidy books on the shelf.

Turn on the television and watch a repeat
Nowhere to go, no-one to meet
Another evening alone things stay the same
Remember the past, relive the pain.

Beans on toast for dinner, it doesn't take long
Put on some music hear the words of a song
Each one refers to a love that's been lost
Love can be bitter as you know to your cost.

Tears flow to your eyes, can't hold them back
Want to act like a man but haven't the knack
To the bathroom you go, in the mirror you look
Wipe tears from your eyes, go pick up a book.

Sit there and read feeling so lost inside
Not quite so tense now that you've cried
Have a few drinks to loosen the mind
A Bacardi with coke or vodka with lime.

Times dragging on and eyes start to droop
Put down the book and to bed you now troop
Sleep doesn't come easy, often disturbed
By activity of mind you find hard to curb.

Up at half six, go to work for your cash
Rain pouring down as to the bus stop you dash
Enter the factory walls painted dull grey
Mirroring how you'll feel by the end of the day.

Go onto the shop floor many people around
Still you feel lonely despite all the sound
For when the working day stops, you're well aware
You'll trudge off back home and sit in your chair.

Dad retired and decided to take Mum on a trip to South Africa to visit his brother David and wife, my Aunt June, and their son Shaun. They had emigrated many years previously although their daughter Karen had remained in England to marry. About a year before this trip Dad had taken Mum to see my brother David who was stationed in Germany, to make sure she could cope with flying as she had never been on a plane before. Mum really enjoyed her trip and as Shaun was to marry about a year later, Dad arranged to go back for the wedding and he paid to take Karen and her young son Alex with them as they couldn't afford the airfares. This was typical of my dad's generosity. Sadly both June and Karen were to die from brain tumours during the 80's and Uncle Dave would come back to England to live. Shaun would stay in South Africa with his new wife.

At work re-structuring was happening as my uncle Sid had passed away suddenly and the sections were all re-arranged with Pat, Ken and Arthur now being the three section leaders and me now becoming Arthur's number two. We had also moved into a new building which had no windows and this was the beginning of the decline in my eyesight, as we were also introduced to computers with black screens and green characters. Within a year I was wearing glasses. Boss Syd had been promoted to my father's vacant position, although he only had a couple of years to go until retirement, so we had a new man in charge of the office called John. He had been a surprise choice as he had never been a section leader, but I believe it was on my dad's recommendation that he was offered the position. John was a kind and thoughtful man and a nice change from Syd. I again felt very lucky because I was working with Arthur a man I both respected and liked.

Just after Dad's retirement Peter bought my share of the house and I found a one bedroom flat in London Road, North End which is just outside of Portsmouth city centre. I had a £32,000 mortgage and although you might call the flat a bit of a dump, it was my dump. It was in a house which had been converted into four one bedroom leasehold flats, mine being one of the two on the ground floor. It consisted of a tiny hallway and leading off to the left was what would have been a decent size living room but for the tiny kitchen that took away a proportion of it. When I say tiny, I mean microscopic. There was enough room for a small fridge next to the cooker, one cupboard above the sink and one below. You had to dish up food on the draining board. Off to the right of the hallway was the bedroom, one third of the space occupied by the en-suit bathroom which had no window and, at the time of purchase, no extractor fan. There were no streetlights at the back of the house so when the bedroom curtains were closed it was pitch black, which I didn't mind. Even as a child the darkness never frightened me. Although a far from luxurious flat, it was to provide me with a safe haven during a remarkable period of my life. I was however to have problems with the freeholders who each year would ask for considerable amounts of money for things that they had not done and my sense of justice wouldn't allow me to pay so I was, according to them, building up quite a large debt in owed maintenance.

Other changes were also happening around me. Martin had split from his wife and had started a relationship with Carol who worked in either the Contracts or Projects department, I can't remember which. I must point out at this point that Carol was not the cause of Martin's marriage break. She was a divorced lady with two teenage sons and she was to become a good friend to me and play a significant part in my future. We are still in touch to this day. After a short time Martin moved into Carol's house which was about a ten minute walk from my flat, in an area of Portsmouth called Stamshaw. At this point, with Martin having a new relationship and Paul now having two young boys to keep him busy, my social life had become almost non-existent. The golfing days seemed to have petered out, and to be honest I was just about managing financially now I had the responsibility of my own property and all the bills that came with it. Martin and Paul had replaced the golf with running, as it didn't cost anything and had completed many ten kilometre runs and at least one full marathon. I had given up on football some years earlier because the booze and cigarettes had taken their toll, and my weight had risen to over 13 stone. I had however managed to stop smoking some years earlier, so Carol and I decided we would train for the Portsmouth half marathon. We would train during the early evenings and when the day came we achieved our goal in a fairly reasonable time. It was during these training times that I began to see a different side to Martin. At times his wife had hinted to me that he was not all he seemed to be, and in his time with Carol I saw him vent his anger more than once, something I had not seen in him before. After a short time Carol asked him to leave and he would come to my flat or we would go out for a pint and he would always be asking the same questions...

"Why has she dumped me when I love her so much?"

We were sitting in his car outside my flat one time and he was going on and on for well over an hour asking me the same question when suddenly he paused in mid-sentence, looked at me and said...

"Do you know Derek? I don't let anybody really know me because if they did they wouldn't like me."

I had thought this man one of my best friends for ten years, but the truth was he was not what he seemed, and he was also right I didn't like what I was seeing. It would be fair to say that during our ten year friendship he showed many qualities that I admired, and perhaps many of us hide things about ourselves that we are not proud of, and anyway was I not pretending to be this man of the world, spouting all my father's political views, when really I was probably still a naive child with no actual views of my own.

Life was now becoming routine, rising in the morning and going to work, returning home in the evenings, watching television and going to bed. It had been at least three years since Judy left and although I had not fallen to pieces, I had given up hope of finding that special someone who I could share my life with. I was lonely and that was a very painful feeling. I would come home some evenings, close the curtains sit on my sofa and cry, simply because I felt empty inside. Carol did her best for me, inviting me down for dinner and on one occasion she talked me into going to a singles night. She drove me to the venue and made sure I went through the door, but once inside I purchased a drink and just sat on my own as others formed into groups, chatting and dancing. At one point a lady came over to me and asked if I'd like to join their table, but I just blushed and said I wasn't ready yet. After all I had no real conversation and no confidence, so eventually I sneaked out and caught the bus home back to the sanctuary of my flat. I had reached the point where I could be in a room full of people and still feel totally lost, just like the little boy who stood in the corner of the room at those Boxing Day parties thirty years previous.

Since moving out I would always make sure that I visited my parents at least once a fortnight and weekly if I could manage it. When Dad was there I would mow the lawn for him as he was beginning to have problems with one of his knees and his mobility was in decline. Peter was working away much of the time and quite often Dad would be over at the Baptist church attending meetings or helping out in some way or another. He had told me that after a few months of retirement he was feeling as if he had lost his way and life had no real use for him, so one day when he was out shopping and feeling quite low he had sent up a thought, Lord I need you to show me the way. That very evening there was a knock on the door and when he opened it a lady was standing there trying to recruit volunteers to help at the Baptist church, the same church I had been to as a member of The Boys Brigade. This had been his salvation and he soon found himself on the church committee. Quite often he would be at the church when I arrived and I would get time to talk to my mother. She would say how pleased she was that he had found something which gave him purpose, but that it wasn't for her and although he had tried to get her involved she had resisted as it wasn't really what she believed in. I sometimes got the feeling I was talking to someone who was as lonely as me but had reached a point in her life when she wasn't able to do anything about it; after all she was now in her early seventies. I suddenly realised that my mother had lived all her adult life as a dutiful wife and mother, just conforming to that role when perhaps her heart and soul had craved much more. I think that this may have been the case for many women of her generation and that makes me sad. For me however, at the age of 35, my life was about to change forever in the most remarkable way.

Chapter Nine: Revelation

"Try this for size, you have two scars on the ...

At the beginning of 1987 my section leader Arthur retired, on his recommendation I was promoted and now ran my own section in charge of six people. Pat walked in one morning, cleared his desk and left. We found out he had cancer and had typically told the doctors that he didn't want any treatment and they should give it to someone that was bothered. They had given him six months, but at Christmas time that year he phoned and asked all of us from his original section to meet him in a pub for a Christmas drink one evening. When we saw him he had lost weight and had a long white beard, but his character had not changed at all and he still ordered five pints of bitter. Six months later we heard of his passing, but at his request none of us were to attend his funeral.

My new section consisted of a man called Chris, promoted from another section as my second in command, Dave who had completed the estimators training course, two other estimators, Andy and John and a clerk, Gary. We made a good team, although I had to keep my eye on Andy because he liked to be over at the bar by 11.30am, would sneak out on the pretext of gathering information, and it would be 1pm before I set eyes on him again. He only had a few years till retirement and lost his wife not long before, so he really didn't care if he had the job or not. But I liked him and he was probably the best mechanical engineer in the department so I couldn't afford to lose him. Gary was a lazy sod who would only do what he had to and could quite often be seen staring into space, even when the pressure was on. At this point, I suppose, you would call me a company man. I would work through lunch hours and till late at night if the job required me to, and the one time I had off sick in ten years was when I was so ill the boss had sent me home. My right hand man Chris, married, with two young children, and Dave, also both had a great work ethic. Now and then the pressures of work would suppress the feelings of loneliness, but I found that you can't hide from emotions for very long and as the months passed I became more and more unhappy. Today that unhappiness might be diagnosed as depression but back then there was a different attitude to such feelings.

After six months I was established in my new role but, away from work, felt I had nothing. That changed when one weekday evening, Carol suddenly asked me...

"Would you like to come to a barbecue Saturday evening?"

"Where's that being held?" I asked.

"At The Temple of Spiritualism in Victoria Road South," she replied.

"How long have you been going there?"

"A few years now, I'm on the committee in a social capacity."

"Thanks for asking Carol but I don't do churches".

"It's only a barbecue; I just thought you might like an evening out."

I paused and thought for a moment. Temple of Spiritualism, what denomination of the Church of England is that? That's how naive I was.

"Ok I'll try it," I said making it sound like I was going to try a new dish in a restaurant.

On the Saturday evening we arrived at this large church building and she guided me through a downstairs room which housed a fair size stage, through to a nice kitchen, into the back garden where several people were gathered. Carol introduced me, everybody was welcoming and to be honest I had a bloody good time. Nobody mentioned God and as we drove home at the end of the evening Carol remarked…

"You appeared to enjoy yourself. We have some sort of a do once a month if you're interested, quiz night, barbecue, or sometimes we put on shows for the older members."

I thought "Why not," and went along to the next two evenings and Carol showed me around the building. Downstairs at the back, behind the stage, was a beautiful healing room which housed several healing couches, while upstairs was the main part of the church with a large raised platform and a small vestry. At the top of the stairs there was a small library from which books could be borrowed. A significant thing I noticed was the building was set back from the road and matched the large Victorian houses that surrounded it, so it didn't stick out like most churches or dominate the skyline as cathedrals do.

It was on my third visit that I first heard the word Medium mentioned and thought: "My god what have I got myself involved in here?"

Almost immediately that thought had passed, this followed: "Everyone you've met seems genuinely to want to help people. You can come here for the nights out, nobody is trying to convert you to anything and if they do you can always say sorry not interested." This was a further distraction from the pain of being a single man craving a partner.

I continued to go each month and nobody tried to convert me or even suggested I go to a church service, but there was one woman who I would occasionally catch staring at me. I had been introduced and knew her name, Pat Pitcher, and was also aware she was a practicing medium, but we had never struck up a conversation, so I didn't think anything of it at the time.

I was at Carol's house one evening when she asked:

"Are you going to come with me to the church tomorrow evening?"

"There's no social tomorrow is there?"

"No, it's a demonstration."

"A demonstration of what?"

"Clairvoyance"

"I'm not into prayers and hymns and all that stuff," I said quickly, trying to end the subject.

"There is an opening and closing prayer but no hymns, it's just a demonstration evening. The Medium is a man from London and is very good, you might just find it interesting and if you don't what have you lost? Just treat it as an evening's entertainment. I'll take you down but I have a committee meeting afterwards so you'll have to make your own way home."

I don't really know what made me agree to go, but I did and I can now say it was the best decision I had ever made in my life – so far.

As I sat at the back of the church, trying to hide behind someone larger than me, I felt excited and at the same time nervous in case this Medium came to me in front of all these people. The first message he gave was to a woman in the front row. I listened intently as she replied to his suggestions with polite one word answers, either yes or no. I remember thinking: "The only way I'm going to know if any of this is really true is if I do get a message myself."

Second message of the evening…

"I want to come to the gentleman at the back who is trying to hide. Yes sir, you wearing the blue shirt;" he said pointing directly at me.

"You know Peter and David and you've lived at a house with the number three. Is that correct sir?"

Well my current address was 321 and my parent's house was 23, so I replied with a yes but thought to myself that most people would know a Peter and David, and many will have lived at an address with a three in the number.

"You can also take the names Gladys and Annie."

"No sorry I can't."

"I'm not convincing you am I sir?" he said.

"I came here with an open mind and I'll probably leave with one;" I replied.

"Try this for size, you have two scars on your left knee and one on your right and the one on your right knee is a half inch below the kneecap."

He didn't even wait for my reply…

"I'll leave you with that sir, god bless."

Well! I nearly fell off my chair and to be quite honest I didn't really hear any more because my mind was racing.

As I left the church to start the half hour walk home I pondered on what had just happened and thought: "There might be something in this, I'd better go and look for myself." This has become a lifelong quest.

During the week I visited my parents and when Dad was out of the room, asked my mother whether there was any family called Gladys or Annie.

"Yes we used to take you to visit Gladys and Reg in Reading when you were a child. Gladys was my cousin and so was Annie who used to live here in Cosham. I used to take you to visit her too but she died when you were very young."

Hmm this gave me more to ponder over.

The following Saturday sitting in Carol's kitchen she asked...

"How did you find the demo last weekend?"

"Interesting," was my one word reply.

"I'm going to the service tomorrow evening if you fancy coming".

"Ok".

At the service I had the strangest feeling of having come home. It wasn't the 40 minutes given over to short messages, it was more the words of the healing hymn and the way the address was given. It wasn't somebody preaching at me, telling me what I had to believe, it was an informal talk which ultimately left me to decide whether it felt right or not, and I have to say for the first time I was at a service which was actually making me feel good. I also read for the first time in the front of the hymn book the seven principles that are the foundation of spiritualism, and they seemed to match the values I had formed within my own life, although it would be fair to say quite often struggled to stick to.

The following Sunday morning I awoke to the sight of a flower pot with one single flower in it floating around my bedroom and watched mesmerised for at least 30 seconds before it just faded into thin air. It reminded me of the times Dad took us to the circus on Southsea common, the clowns would come out with a joke flower pot and the flower would droop and rise again to fits of laughter from the audience. That morning, the service at the Temple was taken by Sue, who I had met with her husband Richard at the social evenings, and Pat Pitcher the lady I had often seen staring at me. Sue did the address and Pat the clairvoyant messages. Morning services lasted an hour and were held downstairs on the last Sunday of the month so disabled people could come. When it had finished, I went to Pat and told her about the flower pot. She said...

"That's spirit showing you what is possible, now you have to go and work for it."

I left wondering how I had to work for it, and at 6.30pm found myself at the evening service watching one of the best clairvoyant displays I have ever seen. At the end of the service Pat came down from the platform and straight over to me...

"I feel inclined to tell you that the church president is going to start a beginners circle in January and you will be offered a place which I feel it would be good for you to accept. If you would like to write any questions down and come to my home one evening I will try to answer them for you. Here is my address and telephone number;" she said, handing me a pre-written piece of paper.

As she walked away, I could see the president making his way over to me. To this day I don't know if I was offered the place on her recommendation or if it was the president's own decision, but whichever it was, I started sitting in circle on the first Monday evening in January 1988.

Just before my first circle I took my questions down to Pat and we did not stop talking from the moment I stepped through her front door. I say we but it was mostly she and, I was to discover that if they gave out Olympic medals for talking, Pat would win the gold every time. She had been born in the USA in August 1947. Her mother was originally from Somerset but had married an American soldier and returned with him at the end of the war. He was apparently of Italian descent, perhaps accounting for Pats olive skin tone. After problems in the marriage her mother came back to Somerset when Pat was 11 and took up with a man called John. They never married, as Pat's mother never divorced her husband, although Pat did consider John to be her stepfather. Pat said she would never forgive her mother for leaving her father. The upheaval affected her quite badly throughout her life. Pat had gone into nursing from school, married and moved to Portsmouth because of her husband's work. After the marriage failed because of his infidelity, Pat got a job running a home for people with Alzheimer's, but was left unemployed when National Health budget cuts led to the home closing down. As we talked I could feel the beginnings of a life-long friendship. By the time she asked for my questions she had already answered them all.

Chapter Ten: Training Begins

"Nobody can sack me for giving an opinion"...

At work things were changing rapidly and I was not doing myself any favours, but outside work I was getting more and more proof that life went beyond the death of the physical form. In the first two months of the New Year I was often supposed to be taking estimates up to meetings with the managing director on Monday evenings, which would mean I would have to miss circle. On each occasion John would call me into the office late in the afternoon and tell me that there was no need for me to stay as he could see the jobs through, so I found I was always able to attend circle. Then something happened at work which solved the problem. I was given the task of producing a very large estimate in seven days. Chris put off his family holiday to help me and, working very long hours we managed to get the job done in the timescale. Soon after, I was sitting at my desk when the phone rang. It was Lyn, Chris's wife and she said...

"Hello Derek, is Chris there please?"

"No I'm afraid he's out of the office at the moment, can I give him a message?" I replied.

"Could you tell him I'm at the hospital and my father has just died?"

"Oh I'm sorry to hear that Lyn, as soon as he comes back I'll send him up to you".

"Thank you".

Chris appeared a few minutes later and I told him to leave his desk and go to the hospital and I would get him a passout for the day. Passouts were short forms that allowed you time off for dental or doctor's appointments or emergencies. Chris shot off and I put his desk in order and went in to see John to tell him what had happened and get him to sign a passout.

"No problem Derek, I'll go straight to Personnel and put the request in for a full day".

John was gone about ten minutes and when he came back he told me that Chris couldn't have a passout as it wasn't his father so he would have to take a day of his annual leave. Fuming does not really describe how angry I was and I set about venting it by writing a letter to the head of Personnel, copied to John and the company chief estimator Ray. The letter told Personnel that their morals stank and that they had not even looked at Chris's records, which showed he never went sick and had cancelled holidays to complete jobs when required. I hand delivered this to all three offices and waited for the fallout. It only took about half an hour...

"Derek, can you come into the office please?"

I walked in and closed the door.

"I've just had the head of Personnel on the phone asking me who the hell you are and saying that he wants to sack you," John told me.

"Tell him from me that no one can sack me for giving an opinion," I replied, then turned and walked out of the office back to my desk.

Shortly afterwards I received an envelope from Personnel and all it contained was a copy of the companies rules regarding bereavements. Perhaps I should have left it there but the sense of injustice was so strong that I marched back into John's office and stated...

"None of this is aimed at you personally, you are a good boss to work for and this used to be a good company with good morals of give and take, but it's now all take. My contract says I work from 8.30 in the morning and finish at 4.30 in the evening, so I'm just letting you know that that is precisely what I shall be doing from now on. If I am required at meetings elsewhere then those meetings will have to be arranged so that my travelling time is taken into consideration, as I won't be leaving before 8.30 and I won't be getting home any later than 4.30. Furthermore if I am at any meetings in the factory I will be leaving them at 4.30."

John looked at me and knew that I was deadly serious. I left the office. Still, at least there was no chance of me missing circle now. From that moment on John never asked me to attend another afternoon meeting or travel anywhere.

Circle was going well and would consist of a 30 minute meditation and then we would all share what we had seen and felt. After this everyone would try to get messages for each other. We were told that everyone had a main guide or doorkeeper and that he or she was your protector but that others from spirit would come in to help in your development when necessary. I had been told that I had a North American Indian as my main guide and been given the name of Grey Bear by one of the other members of the circle. I was beginning to meditate at home now in the evenings and starting to form a relationship with my guide, without really understanding where all this was going to lead.

It was mid-September 1988 and I suddenly received a letter from Jenny's mother in which she told me that Jenny and Bill's daughter Lucy had been having treatment for leukaemia, but unfortunately the doctors did not expect her to last the year out. The letter went on to say that they were arranging an early Christmas for Lucy and that she hoped I would understand if there was no card that year. I was devastated for the family and can honestly say that I had never prayed for anything so much as I did for this little girl's life, even though I had never met her. Every night I would send out sincere thoughts and would not stop until eventually I fell asleep. I was to hear no more about Lucy for over a year.

Life continued on all fronts into the New Year. Mum and Dad had taken their second trip to South Africa and had even gone on a short safari whilst they were there. Dad then called a family meeting to tell us they were going to the solicitors to make their wills and he wanted to know what all of us wanted. I think it was a unanimous reply that he had worked hard for the little he had and he and Mum should enjoy it whilst they were alive and not worry about us.

Work was now becoming a big concern for me and I was beginning to question the moral issues concerned with what I was doing. I had also once again put my foot in it big time. As a section we were being overloaded with every emergency job that came into the office. I like to think that that was because we were very good at our job, but the pressure of being delegated so many rush jobs was beginning to get up the noses of my little group. One afternoon they came to me and Chris spoke for them all...

"This is getting too much Del; we seem to be getting all of the rubbish whilst the other sections are only working on single projects."

"I'll take your concerns into John" I replied.

I went into John's office, shut the door and asked if I could have a word.

"Of course, what's the problem?" he asked.

I explained and then he let me have it, both barrels...

"You are a section leader for this company and you should be out there encouraging and boosting morale instead of listening to petty complaints," he shouted at me.

"I can't do that," I said, keeping remarkably calm for me.

"Why can't you?" he raged.

"Because I agree with them," I said calmly, and with that I got up and left. I walked back to my section and asked them to gather around and then I said with my back to the office door...

"I've just taken your concerns into John and been given an earful. Apparently my job is to stop you lot whinging, keep you working hard and boost your morale when you're getting pissed off. So, here is your morale boost... it's Friday and it's now approximately four o'clock and in a half hour you can pack up and get out of this shithole and you don't have to come back until Monday."

I heard the office door slam shut behind me.

I was still having moments of feeling lonely but less so now that I had spirit to commune with, however, I still craved that one-on-one relationship. In the Temple I had become involved in the organisation of the monthly entertainment, but was also beginning to understand that the same corrupt practises I had seen in all the other churches were also to be seen here. The minister and the president didn't want change and would use unfair tactics to make sure that anybody who was nominated to contest for president would fail. I also noticed that after each service people would be rushing over to each other to give messages and this had happened to me on numerous occasions. I would receive a message from the visiting Medium, usually giving me good advice about my spiritual progression and then two or three people; most of whom I had never met would rush over to me at the end of the service and, without asking if I would take a message from them, would pour out a load of garbage. When you go to a service you are giving the visiting Medium permission to come to you but you are not giving others that right.

I had also started to attend a few full day workshops to try to learn a bit more and to see how different Mediums worked and how different practices fitted into the process, Chinese face reading, Tarot, and Colour to name a few. One of these workshops was taken by Mavis Patilla, a prominent northern Medium who was to say something very significant to me and I have never forgotten it. There were about 25 of us at her workshop, all sitting in a circle and Mavis started by asking us all to introduce ourselves and say why we were there. The first 20 or so had spoken when it came to my turn I began to introduce myself...

"My name is Derek and I'm here to learn more about this process and..."

"Sorry to interrupt you" she said, "but when you started to speak your aura just increased and shone so brightly that I must say to you I have not seen potential like yours before. When you have developed your clairvoyance you should not stop there, but go on to develop trance. Please remember though that I have used the word potential, and that you must be prepared to work hard to fulfil it."

1989 ended with the collapse of the Berlin Wall and more great news when I received a Christmas card from Jenny's mother which said, and I quote... "Lucy is fine PTL". It took me weeks to work out that PTL meant Praise the Lord.

Chapter Eleven: Commitment

"Go away; fuck off and come back later...

With the collapse of the wall defence contracts also fell. The company began to branch out into the commercial world of mobile phones and other small electronic gadgets and my section was to deal with these contracts. This went someway to quelling my moral concerns; in fact the year was to be quite a quiet one for me in work considering the earlier conflicts. Redundancies came in the first half of the year, but they affected the manufacturing side rather than us in the offices, although there was the threat of more to follow.

My Monday circle continued although I was beginning to feel I wasn't really going anywhere and everything seemed to be at a bit of a crossroads. Apart from my experience with the first message and the flowerpot, I had one other happening in meditation, when a man who looked just like the form of Jesus that you see in paintings and books came and sat next to me and held my hand. Other than that it was the giving and receiving of very vague messages during circle.

There was worry in the family as war started in the gulf and David was sent out to work in a desert hospital. I started to correspond with him and he later told me how grateful he was to receive my letters. The nightly news reports were painting a very bloody picture and, although my parents never said so, I could tell they were worried for his safety.

In November I was talking to Carol when she said...

"There is a demo evening this Saturday if you're interested. The Medium is a young man called Neil from London, who we have never had at the Temple before, and I'm hosting him for the weekend."

"Hosting him, what does that entail?" I asked.

"Putting him up and feeding him. I've just agreed to do it as they don't have enough people willing to," she replied. "If you come here at about six, we can travel down together."

I arrived at Carols at six and we made our way into her large kitchen where I parked my backside at the breakfast bar. She looked at me and said…

"He's upstairs having a shower. He's a young man but a bit strange and he told me you were coming tonight."

"What do you mean he told you I was coming?"

"He walked in and said,' Hello Carol, nice to meet you and thanks for putting up with me for the weekend. I hope you and the young man will enjoy the evening'."

There was the sound of footsteps on the stairs and then Neil appeared. As he sat down, he looked at me and said…

"Hello Derek, I won't shake your hand, I'm recovering from a slipped disc so I need to just sit here a while before we leave. It's going to be a good night tonight."

I greeted him and turned to finish the coffee Carol had made me. She looked at me and mouthed…

"I didn't tell him your name."

Now normally I would have questioned that, but I had now known Carol for some years and had never known her to lie.

Suddenly Neil began talking quietly to himself and I heard him say…

"Go away; fuck off and come back later when I'm at the church."

My immediate thought was, ding dong pull the other one.

He continued to talk to himself until we left for the church and I was beginning to regret saying I would go.

It was cold, dark and pouring with rain and as seven o'clock approached there were only seven of us there with Neil. Carol and I, Gary and his wife Kay, Malcolm and his wife Joyce and the church minister Lawry. By now I was familiar with all of these people and felt quite comfortable around them. Kay and Gary had become good friends and when, in the following few years, they had their two girls Heather and Becky, I was to be a willing babysitter.

"I'm not doing a bloody demonstration for seven people, we'll close the doors at five past and go into the vestry and I'll do a trance talk," Neil stated.

Everyone but me seemed quite excited by this.

So there we all were in the vestry, sitting in a circle, and I found myself sitting to the right hand side of Neil. I remember looking at the clock as he closed his eyes and went into what I now know was a light trance and it was just before ten past seven. After a few minutes he began to talk about the fall of the wall and the differences it was making to the structure of societies. I don't remember all the things he said, I just remember that I didn't take my eyes off of him and I was totally enthralled. After about ten minutes Lawry, obviously not as enrapt as I was, yawned and looked at his watch and Neil, without opening his eyes pointed at him and said...

"Don't do that, don't you ever do that, I don't work to time and nor do spirit. I'll have your watch stopped now and that clock stopped," pointing to the large clock on the vestry wall.

I have no idea if Lawry's watch stopped but the vestry clock stopped immediately, never working again and replaced about two years later. My stomach was churning as he continued speaking for some time and then opened his eyes and asked if anyone had questions. I was still gobsmacked by the clock stopping but the others had either seen this sort of thing before or hadn't noticed, so they began to ask questions. After answering these he said…

"I suppose I've got to give everyone a message now. This is not what it's all about."

He started with Gary who was sitting opposite me and began to work his way around the circle and everyone was saying yes to him until he came to Lawry, who gave more negative answers than positive. As he began to talk to Carol who was sitting next to me I began to send up nervous thoughts, don't come to me, I don't want it in front of these people.

Because I knew Carol pretty well at that point I knew that everything he was saying to her was true. When he had finished he then turned his head away and said…

"That's enough; I'm going back to Carol's now for a curry. We can get a curry near your place Carol can't we?"

"Yes" she replied.

"Good, come on let's go, I'll talk to Derek later. "

With that we left, drove to the Indian restaurant and bought his curry, which If my memory serves me right was a Chicken Madras, took him back to Carol's where he proceeded to devour it. When he had finished he placed his knife and fork on the plate and pushed it to one side. Carol moved towards the table to collect the plate but he beckoned to her to stay where she was, and then he started on me, 45 minutes in which he told me things about my life that I had shared with no-one, and I mean no-one, but it was the really trivial things that caught my attention. I had no washing machine at home so every Thursday evening I would leave my washing at the launderette which was only a minute walk from my flat. In that washing were my shirts for work, and after picking the washing up each Friday evening I would immediately iron my shirts for the following week. For several weeks I had been thinking to myself that I desperately needed to buy some new shirts as the collars were in a very poor condition. I also had a habit of taking my loose change from my pocket and throwing it down next to the television or onto the coffee table and that very morning I had quickly been to buy a new pair of shoes which I was not wearing that night and had not told anyone about simply because to us men a pair of shoes is a pair of shoes.

"Your Grandfather's standing behind you holding up shirts to the light and says, yes boy you do need new shirts, and will you stop throwing your money about when you get home from work. If you had to work as hard as he did for it you would hang on to it tightly. He's also not keen on the shoes you've just bought. He says you should have proper shoes with laces not the slip on rubbish."

At this point he had me, and I just sat there and listened...

"Did you know you had five brothers and sisters in spirit?"

"No I haven't."

I had a very faint memory of my mother talking to a neighbour about miscarriages when I was a child, but I didn't remember who they were talking about and at that age I probably wouldn't have known what a miscarriage was.

"Yes you have. Ask your mother, and by the way the partner you crave will find you, you don't have to look, and when it happens you won't believe your luck, and others will be envious of your relationship. Also tell your mother that the sailor man says hello, and that the young man who is away at the moment will return safely but he will be a different character because of what he has seen."

After a few more things about changes to my working environment he stood up, offered me his hand to shake and finished with...

"Oh and by the way you'll be doing what I do and you'll do it better that me."

He sat back down and then enquired...

"What's this business about the young man?"

I told him about David and he looked straight at me and asked...

"So Derek; if I was an Iraq soldier standing here what would you do?"

Without hesitation I replied: "I'd shoot you."

"Why?"

"Because if I don't you might go on to kill fifty of my mates or comrades."

"Are you happy with that answer?"

"Yes," I replied

"Ok, but I will tell you that I wouldn't shoot him. I won't tell you why but somebody else will very soon."

With that we adjourned to the front room because there was a film coming on that he wanted to watch. After the film I made my way home, promising to go to the evening service the following day.

Chapter Twelve: Confirmation and Acceptance

"Ok, if you want me to do this then you teach me…

It was Sunday morning and I was buying my food for the following week in the local supermarket, about a half mile walk from my flat. This was part of my normal Sunday routine, as close to the supermarket was a nice coffee shop where I would stop on my walk back home to read my Sunday newspaper whilst indulging in a toasted sandwich and a couple of milky coffees. I had paid at the tills and just exited the large doors at the front of the supermarket, with a bag of shopping in each hand, when suddenly a voice from outside my right ear said…

"It is not your responsibility my son."

"Do what!" I said out loud, and people stared at me which made me feel very uncomfortable and embarrassed but, as I started to go red in the face, the voice repeated…

"Not your responsibility he kills fifty others, he answers for that not you, you answer if you kill him."

I didn't stop at the coffee shop that morning. I went straight home, placed my shopping by the side of the sofa and sat trying to find a contradiction to the statement made and I couldn't. Furthermore, as someone who was beginning to believe in the eternal existence of the soul, the truths held within that statement were to lead my thoughts in many other directions. At that moment something inside me changed. Just a single sentence from an unseen source had set me on a path of discovery, not just the discovery of spirit but the discovery of me and what I truly believed.

That evening I went to the service that Neil was taking. When he stood up to start the messages which are meant to prove life after death, his first message was interrupted as the doors to the church opened and an elderly man supported by two younger men walked through and sat in the back row of seats. Neil paused whilst this was happening and, then turned to the woman he was engaged with and said...

"Excuse me for just a minute, I promise I will come back to you, but there is something I must do."

Turning his attention to the elderly gentleman, he gently said...

"Doris is ok my friend, she has made her transition and is resting with those that love her. She has no pain now and her thoughts and love are for you and your sons."

I have to say here that I have put the name Doris because he did give a name, but I have no recollection of what it was.

The gentleman whispered a thank you through his tears and the three of them stood up and walked from the church. As they left I heard one of the ushers ask...

"Would your father like to sit downstairs for a while and can I get him some water or a cup of tea?"

One of the young men replied...

"No thank you, he's got what he came for."

They were not in the church for more than three minutes.

Neil went back to the lady and continued the service.

When we were back at Carol's I told Neil what had happened that morning and he only said one sentence...

"Good, now remember that that was your experience and any experience that follows is yours, nobody else can have it."

That night I went to bed and lay on my back looking up into the darkness and I can't remember if I thought these next words or if I said them out loud, but I do know they were probably the most sincere of my life to that point…

"Ok, if you want me to do this then you teach me. I don't want to read books, it has to come from you because then I'll believe it to be the truth, and if I ever hurt anyone you won't see me for dust."

I had barely finished before my bedroom was a mass of coloured lights with golden figures standing beside the bed. I can't say these figures were in human form or really had any human characteristics, but they were light forms of a human size. The smaller balls of different coloured lights moved around the room fading in and out, changing colour as they did but the most amazing thing to me was that I felt no fear whatsoever, only excitement and anticipation. This kaleidoscope went on for some time before the room was dark and still again and I eventually drifted off to sleep.

The following week I was in a bit of a daze and would rush home from work, close my curtains to shut out the distractions of everyday living and after something to eat I would go to the bedroom and just lie there looking up to the ceiling. The lights would appear and fade in and out as I watched for what seemed like hours. One evening I went to my parent's house and Dad was over at the Baptist church so I got the opportunity to talk to Mum and tell her what Neil had said…

"Who's the sailor man Mum?"

"What sailor man?" she replied looking a bit confused.

"Well, I had this sort of spiritual reading last Saturday and I was told to tell you that the sailor man says hello and also that you're not to worry about David because he will come home safe".

She didn't really reply to the bit about the sailor man, just gave me a knowing smile, and to this day I still wonder what that smile meant.

"Did you lose any children Mum?"

I remember the exact words of her reply...

"Yes, I lost two sets of twins and one other, I could have had a football team."

I have promised to be honest, so at this point in case I forget to tell you later, I must say that sometime in the future after my mother's passing, my father denies this emphatically. It would be fair to say that my father did not agree with what I was getting involved in, but as I understand it my mother had said to him that she thought I had changed for the better because of it, and apparently he didn't deny that this was true.

It took me at least three months to replace the shirts and today I still throw my loose change down as soon as I come home.

Not long after this experience Pat came to me and said...

"I think it's time to move on, there is a place opening up in the home circle I sit in on Sunday evenings after the service has finished. I've spoken to Sue and Richard and they are going to offer you a place."

By now Pat and I were good friends and she had become a mentor to me, so when the offer came I grabbed it. Luckily Kay, who also sat, said she would give me a lift home as we wouldn't start till 9.30 pm, which meant we usually wouldn't leave until after midnight when all the bus services had stopped. Also offered a place was a young man called Kevin who was lodging at Pat's house and had also been sitting with me in the Monday circle. Pat, who had a new addition to her household in the form of a female tortoiseshell kitten called Flora, told Kevin and I that we would have to finish in the Monday circle. Kevin left straight away, but I was scared of upsetting my fellow sitters, so it took me a few weeks to pluck up the courage to leave. Sue and Richard were members of the church, a well-educated couple, who between them store a considerable amount of knowledge. Sue's speciality is astrology and producing astrological charts while Richard is an expert on the history of tarot, or as he entitles his workshops 'The Journey of the Wise Fool'. Pat also said that she thought we should start up a trance circle where Kevin and I could sit for development.

In Sue and Richard's circle both me and a lady called Elizabeth were made to work hard as far as the development of clairvoyance was concerned, although we did have some fun evenings when we would try different things like getting the heavy glass ashtray to move around the table. It would move so fast you could hardly keep your finger on it, and it would come so far off the edge of the table without falling off completely that if one of the others was controlling it then they were bloody good at it. The trance circle had started in the front room of my small flat and had filled the gap on Monday evenings. Pat and her best friend Elen, who was a spiritual healer at the Temple, gave up every Monday evening to help Kevin and I develop, soon to be reduced to just me. For the first six months, all that happened was that Kevin and I would sit in turn for about 45 minutes. Personally, it felt like my consciousness was being controlled and I was in a deep meditative state and other than that nothing seemed to happen, but when I came out of that state Pat and Elen would tell me what they had seen. This was generally, several different faces masking over mine, one of which was a young man with an earring and flat cap. I must say I found it very interesting watching Kevin as I then got to see the different faces appear.

It was during the early months of these new circles that I began to have new experiences at home. One Tuesday morning when I awoke in my small one bedroom flat, a lady walked from the en-suite and passed me as I lay. She turned her head, smiled and without speaking disappeared through the open bedroom door. I remember smiling back before thinking: "Orange top and lime green skirt don't go well together," and then, "Who the fuck are you and what are you doing in my flat?" I leapt from the bed and ran into the living room; she was nowhere to be seen.

I was beginning to get impatient and sending my thoughts to spirit almost pleading with them to speed my development as if I was given the clairvoyant abilities quickly I could actually start to help people. I went to bed one evening sending up these thoughts and had the most realistic dream in which Elizabeth was suddenly given clairvoyance and began to use it, but not in a good way. She began forcing messages of doom and disaster on friends, family and work colleagues without any discipline and I was screaming at her to stop saying: This is not right, you are not helping, just bringing fear to people." At the point of waking I felt as if my whole body, internally, was on fire. This sensation took a few minutes to cease but when it did I looked up into the darkness and said just two words...

"I understand."

That dream taught me a vital lesson which I have tried hard to pass on as I have worked through the past 25 years. Sitting for two hours a week for maybe 45 weeks of the year equates to approximately eleven working days of eight hours. Would you let an electrician re-wire your house, or a plumber put in your heating system, if they had done just eleven days training? Most apprenticeships take four years of working at least five days a week, for eight hours a day, before a trainee is considered qualified and even then improvement only comes with the continual practice of that skill. I was soon to get confirmation that this dream was indeed a lesson to be learnt when a few days later I visited Carol and found her in somewhat of a dilemma. She had been tidying the boys' rooms, come across a small amount of cannabis and was worried that this might be a starting point to stronger drugs. Both the boys were out but due back within the hour for dinner, so she decided to call the police and ask them to come and give the boys a warning. When the boys came home a big burly policeman arrived at the door and gave them a stern reprimand before taking the cannabis and leaving. They were both angry and stormed out calling their mother all sorts of names, which naturally upset her. They hadn't been gone long when the phone rang, she picked it up but before she could say a word Neil's voice came bellowing down the line...

"I know what's just gone on in your house Carol and I want you to know that getting the police was the right thing to do. I know Derek is there so tell him that his dream was a message from spirit and he has no need to rush, the work will appear for him when he is ready." Then he just put the phone down on her.

Pat had started her own development circle, to be held at Elen's house every Thursday evening, and both Elen and I were to help and learn how to run a circle properly. A few months earlier my sister, worried about what I was getting into had gone to the Temple herself, and to cut a long story short had come to the same conclusions I had, and she and her husband Andy came to sit in Pat's circle. On the first evening we had about seven others sitting but it became clear after a few weeks that two of our sitters were only there in the hope of getting messages each week, so Pat gave Elen and I the task of each telling one of these that they were not ready to sit and therefore could no longer come to circle. This was not because she wasn't prepared to do this herself, but to teach us that you must achieve the right balance of people, all of whom must be ready to sit. One of the other sitters was a lovely lady called Enid who was quite involved with the high Anglican Church and many of her friends were Anglican ministers. She said she had come because she wanted to see if she could marry the two spiritual concepts together as she had read many books on the subject of Spiritualism. Enid had two grown up children and lived in Stamshaw, not far from Carol. From Monday to Friday she would live in Portsmouth but every Friday evening she would take the ferry across to France to spend the weekend with her husband who worked there. I will speak of Enid again later in my story. Pat told me that it was time to practice giving readings, starting with friends who would understand if I was hesitant, and that it was for development purposes only.

Six months in and we were sitting at Sue and Richard's when they asked Kevin to practice his clairvoyance. He closed his eyes and to the surprise of everybody he looked as if he was going into trance. He then suddenly boomed out in a strange voice...

"Hello."

Richard replied: "Hello friend can you tell us your name?" Kevin raised his hand, pointed towards Pat, and in the same booming voice said...

"She knows who I am."

I looked at Pat and her face confirmed everything I was feeling, this was fake. My heart sank, Pat just sat there not speaking and I could see she was angry. Her silence spoke volumes and Kevin must have sensed something because he didn't utter another word, just opened his eyes and carried on the pretence by rubbing his eyes and saying how strange he had felt. As we left the house I whispered to Pat...

"I'm sorry but I can't be a part of that."

"Good, I'm pleased you are able to tell when something is not right Derek, don't worry I will get this sorted," she whispered back.

As I understand it when she and Kevin got home she sat him down and told him straight, and then told him that he should go to his room each evening and make his links with those from spirit who worked with him. After two evenings he came to her and said that it wasn't for him as it was all taking too long and he wanted to drop out of both circles. Soon afterwards he left Pat's and moved to London, so the trance circle was now just the three of us. After Kevin left things began to take a step forward as spirit began to move my hands and open my mouth as if preparing me to speak. When they opened my mouth it would remind me of the cocaine injections I used to have at the dentist that would spread all over my tongue. Sometimes they would stand me up and walk me to the door and then return me to the chair and sit me down again. If you've ever raised yourself from an armchair with your eyes shut, walked somewhere, returned and sat down again without using your hands, then you will know how difficult this is. It was all done so gently and as I sat back down it was as if the bottom half of my body was being gently cradled until I was back in the chair. Before I was given back control, each part of me that had been moved was placed in the same position it had started from.

Spirit were now supplying me with all the confirmation I required and I was now accepting and trusting all that was happening, although I did fail on one occasion.

For some time I had also been having a strange experience at home which I don't really know how to put into words but am going to try. In the evenings, when I had finished dinner, I would lie on my bed and practise blanking my mind as I thought this would help with both the clairvoyance and trance training. This had reached a point where I would get a high pitched frequency in my ears which would seem to get higher and higher until I thought my consciousness was going to open up completely, but then anxiety would set in and the sound would recede. For months I had been trying to pluck up the courage to take it beyond the point where fear took over, but had never managed to do so. One evening I had been in bed for only a few minutes not really thinking of anything when the frequency began to build, and this time I found the courage to let it go beyond the usual point. The only way I can describe it is that it felt as if the inside of my head was empty of any matter and there was a rushing sound, like a strong breeze spiralling through my mind, and on that breeze a clear soft voice was calling my name…" Derek, Derek." I answered out loud…

"Yes, yes," and then almost in panic: "No, no I'm not ready for this," at which point the breeze receded taking the voice with it. I have always wondered if that was my doorway to actually having spirit voice talking to me instead of everything working through thought patterns. I have tried to attain that feeling again many times since but never succeeded.

Chapter Thirteen: Cleansing

"You always said you'd never have a ginger headed child...

I was coming to the realisation that to be a good and honest channel for my god source I really had to look at myself, but this process was very difficult because it meant admitting I was wrong in much of my thinking. It made me realise that I was as much to blame for the breakdowns of my two serious relationships as the girls were, if not more so. Being a lapdog in order to keep someone just made me boring, and just doing anything to please without having any point of view was pathetic. In spouting off the politics of my father I was saying things, I didn't actually believe as I had never really questioned them, because they had been drilled into me. As difficult as this process was and indeed still is, for it is always work in progress, it is a process that has come to define me as a person and brought me to a place where I can now truly say: "I like who I am."

Very quickly in the process two things happened. I decided to write to Jenny's mother to ask if Jenny would accept a letter from me and received a letter back saying she would as long as it was passed through her mother. I duly wrote and apologised for the terrible things I had said, and extended my wish that she and her family would always be happy and at peace. I received a beautiful reply saying we were both at fault, thanking me for my words and hoping that I was now happy. It may be strange to say but it felt as if a burden had been lifted from me, even stranger however, was one evening that same week my doorbell rang and when I opened it there stood Judy with a young ginger headed boy.

"Hello Derek, I hope you don't mind but I got your address from Sonia."

Sonia was a girl who worked in the drawing store at Marconi and, had also played in the same ladies darts team as Judy.

"No, come in," I replied, frantically trying to work out the age of the boy and realising by the time we reached the front room that he was too young to be mine. She told me she had gone to London and, within a few weeks, left her boyfriend who had gone back to heavy gambling. She then moved to Birmingham, met and married a Brummie, and was now in Portsmouth to visit her parents. She saw I was having trouble not laughing and asked why?

"You always said you'd never have a ginger headed child," I said grinning.

She just laughed whilst her son jumped all over my furniture.

"Mum's having the boy this evening and I'm going to Sonia's for a drink and catch up. Would you like to come with me? I'm only here for a couple of days and I'd like to know how things have turned out for you," she said.

"Ok," I replied.

Sonia lived within walking distance from my flat, so Judy left her car at her mum's, caught the bus to mine at seven and we made our way there. The evening went well, a couple of bottles of wine were drunk and the time of the last bus had passed as Judy and I made our way back to my flat. I could tell from the conversation that she did not want to go back to her parents that night and expected to stay with me. Probably at any earlier time of my life I would have succumbed to the temptation, after all I was very lonely and a night in the arms of an attractive woman would have been very welcome, but I took her into the flat, phoned a taxi and sent her on her way. A one night stand was not what I wanted apart from which, morally, I knew I had done the right thing.

I was also beginning to look deeply at all of the views of my father that I was repeating ad hoc, discovering flaws in the logic and substance of them, and realising I had no real opinions of my own. Here I was a 37 year old man as shallow as a brook; politically, socially and emotionally inept, but it may be true to say that even the process of discovering this was a move in the right direction.

Sue had set up a class at the church called Platform Presentation, aimed at those that might one day take services or take part in demonstration evenings. Sue's day job was as a music teacher in a school, but she was also a semi-professional singer used to stage appearances, so she was well qualified to help others to project their voices in large halls so that everyone would be able to hear what was being said. I was on the downstairs stage one evening, practising an address, when the doors opened and in walked a couple who had come to join the class. As they walked towards the stage, suddenly the gentleman stopped in his tracks and stared straight at me. I stopped in mid-flow, stared back and recognition hit us both at the same time. It was Alan, my charge hand from over fifteen years earlier at Frater. I jumped down from the stage and walked over to him hand outstretched and he took it and shook whilst saying…

"My god, this is the last place in the world I ever thought I would have bumped into you."

"Ditto," I replied and we both laughed.

We sat down and, over cups of coffee, reminisced about the past and our arguments like we were old buddies. As we did, it seemed as if all of the animosity just disappeared and a mutual respect was being formed. Alan and his wife were to go on to run Havant Spiritualist Church where I was to serve many times, and in all the following years, even though we may still have thought differently on many subjects, my respect for him and his point of view grew and I think and hope he might say the same of me.

At home I was to have another wonderful experience. I can't remember where I had been but I arrived home late one evening and after a quick drink took myself off to bed. I hadn't been in bed long when out of the corner of my eye I could see flickering light on the wall to the left. I turned my head to look directly at the wall and it was as if the reflection of flames were shooting up it from floor to ceiling. It took me a few seconds to realise what I was seeing and from the corner of my other eye I could make out flickering light from the gap at the bottom of my bathroom door. I shot out of bed thinking there was a fire in the bathroom and did what you should never do; I flung the bathroom door open. Nothing, just darkness and then the bedroom went dark as the flickering on the wall stopped. As I walked back to the bed I said...

"If that's you, do it again."

I had hardly got the words out when the reflection of flames shot up the wall, lighting up the whole room. It lasted just a few seconds before everything fell into darkness again and I climbed back into bed giggling to myself.

Another cleansing process was about to happen but this time in my working environment. There had already been a second wave of redundancies and talk was that a third would be happening in the middle of the following year. It was approaching the end of 1991 and I was sitting at my desk beavering away, when a young girl appeared next to me. She placed a document in front of me and said...

"Hi, I'm from Personnel, will you sign this for me please?"

"What is it?" I enquired.

"It's just a form to change your job title."

"Why? I'm sorry but I don't understand."

"You are no longer Section Leader; you are now Chief Estimator of the Commercial Division."

I picked up the document and read the first few lines and sure enough there I was now a chief estimator. I handed it to the girl and asked...

"Can you point to the part that tells me what my new salary is please?"

"Oh, there's no rise in pay," she said, placing the form back in front of me.

"I'm sorry then, but I'm not signing it."

"Everyone else has signed their forms, you're the last one."

"I'm sorry, but I won't be signing it today."

With that she picked it up and headed straight for John's office. A few minutes later she walked back past me and left, minus the form. John called me in and asked, in a somewhat pleading manner...

"Are you going to sign this Derek?"

"No I'm not John. From what I've read this change means more responsibility, and yet there is no pay rise and no one has actually been bothered to ask me if I want the job. There's been no interview or consultation with me whatsoever."

"Sign it now and I'll do my best to get you a rise a little later," he said.

"I've no doubt you will try John, but we both know that it ain't gonna happen."

I left the office feeling a little sorry for him because he was a genuine man and I know he would have tried, but I also knew he would fail. A little later he came over to me and told me that he and I had an interview with the commercial manager, at noon the following day, to discuss my refusal to sign. That evening I began to churn over in my mind what I was going to say at the meeting and the more I thought about it the angrier my scenarios became. I went to bed with the idea that I was going to tell the commercial manager exactly what I thought, in no uncertain terms. I drifted off to sleep with anger in my heart. I awoke in the early hours of the morning needing the bathroom and, after relieving the pressure on my bladder, was walking back to bed when, for the second time, a voice outside my right ear clearly said…

"You should learn to quell anger my son, stay calm, compromise and remember it is not your place to judge, not even when it concerns you."

I went back to bed with these words replaying in my head and woke the following morning with a great sense of calm. At midday John and I walked into the commercial manager's office, sat at the end of a huge conference table, and I could see he had the form in front of him.

"Now what's this all about Derek, why won't you just sign the form and accept the new position?"

Very calmly I asked: "Does this new position increase my responsibilities and, if it does, where are the rewards that go with those extra responsibilities? After all, we all come to work to improve our quality of life and to earn the capability to do so."

He countered: "Yes, of course it does, but we don't know if you are capable of doing the job until you actually do it."

"That is true of anyone in any position, even yours, but I very much doubt you signed your contract before you knew what salary you were going to get and, furthermore, I doubt your job was thrust upon you without you actually having been interviewed or in fact even applying for the position," I replied.

He seemed taken aback by this and before he could speak I calmly added…

"Look, let me make this easy for everyone, I don't want the position so by all means offer it to someone else."

He turned to John and said…

"I don't think there's any more to be said John, thank you both for coming."

I got up and left them at the table and made my way to the canteen for lunch. When I returned John called me into his office…

"Well, I've never seen anything like that before, when you left he told me he was seeing you in a completely different light and that he thought the best thing to do was to leave things exactly as they are."

Big lesson learnt on the anger management side and, more importantly, that these principles were not only for others but applied to me as well.

Chapter Fourteen: Lessons and Proof From Practice

"Perfection for whom Derek, you or her...

As part of my practice I had been talked into putting up a reading as a raffle prize at one of the monthly entertainment evenings and it was won by a young girl who I had never met before. Somebody who knew her told me that she was a budding Medium who sat in circle at Havant Church, so I thought to myself: "She'll just want to know about her progression and the guides and helpers that are around her." When she came to the flat I did her reading and she seemed thrilled with what had been given and went away very happy. I then sat down to say thank you to Grey Bear and those that had come to speak, but when I closed my eyes the power to send out thoughts was completely taken from me, just as it was when I sat for trance development. I was then gently, but firmly, reprimanded with my guide telling me that I had decided what messages she needed and, that although all I had given was correct, I had blocked anything that didn't suit the type of message I thought she required. I was told that her mother would have liked to have spoken to her but because I was so intent on giving only what I wanted to, I had blocked her from coming through. This came as a great shock to me and I immediately phoned Pat to tell her what had happened.

"You must phone her up, admit your failing and ask her to come again so that her mother's message, along with anything else you've blocked out, can be given," she told me.

I must say I found this very difficult to do, but I did do it. She was most surprised and told me not to worry as she had been pleased with what she had been given, but we agreed a new date, and when she came, the message from her mother was a very significant one.

During those entertainment evenings I met a girl called Karen. Karen was full of life, and still is for that matter, but what I mean is she was the total opposite of me, outgoing, hugely entertaining with a very distinct sense of humour. I was later to learn that she is from a large Irish family and has five sisters and two brothers. In August 1991 Karen asked if she and her husband Chris could come for a reading, so we arranged an evening that suited us both. I will tell you at this point that I have their permission to share the most significant part of their reading with you, which is something I will not do with most of the other readings I may mention. Most of the information given was from Chris's grandfather, Thomas, but during the reading the following words were said...

"You will have the child you want, you'll know by the end of January, and for some reason I have to say it will be natural."

When I had finished Karen said...

"We can take all of that Derek except the bit about natural childbirth because I don't ovulate, so I've been having IVF treatment which we've just stopped because it is so expensive, so I'm afraid what you say isn't likely."

"Oh I'm sorry to hear that, but I can't take it back because if I do I don't have a right to do this," I replied.

They left and I wondered how I'd interpreted what I was getting so wrongly, yet when I closed my eyes to thank spirit there was no rebuke.

About a week later a lady phoned saying she had been given my number by the Church and could she come and see me, so not wanting to turn down an opportunity I said yes. This was to lead to another significant lesson. The lady came and after the reading she said she could take most of what was given, but that I hadn't sorted out the main problem which involved her son and the police. When she left and I closed my eyes, I sent my thoughts to spirit and told them that it wasn't good enough, I hadn't been able to sort this lady's problem and if I was going to do this it had to be perfect. The moment I had finished my ability to think was again taken from me and my guide's words began to fill my head once again...

"Perfection for whom Derek, you or her; we cannot take away her or her son's learning process, that's not what this is about. It is her that matters and you must trust that what we give is perfect for that person at that time, so learn now that perfection may not be what you think it is, and what is perfect for one may not be what is perfect for another."

He was right, I had to trust and I also had to leave my ego out of it.

Lessons were now coming thick and fast. Spirit were certainly doing their best to keep to their side of the agreement and I was about to undergo two more personal experiences. I had become friendly with a girl at work, Carolyn, who had been transferred to Portsmouth from Chelmsford to sort out a particular problem with a job I had been involved in. Carolyn had got involved with a man who worked on the shop floor and it was, to say the least, a very troubled relationship because he kept on calling it off and then relighting the fire and she didn't know where she stood. I somehow had become her first point of call for each time the relationship went pear-shaped. She called me one night at about eleven and I was on the phone for over two hours as she unburdened herself. I tried to put the sensible side of the situation, but to no avail and when I came off of the phone, went to my bed and began to sob uncontrollably. As I was crying I was thinking: "What the hell are you crying for Derek," but I couldn't stop. From my window came a light translucent blue mist which began to spread and fill my bedroom, engulfing me as I wept, and as it did all my emotions flooded from me and I felt as if I was held in complete and unconditional love. A voice then spoke to me in my head saying...

"You have taken on all of her problems and now you must release them because they are not yours. You must learn what is yours to deal with and what is not, so that you can stay objective and always give the correct advice not tainted by emotion. What your heart may wish for someone may not always be what is best for them."

When my sobbing ceased the blue mist slowly dispersed until my room was dark again.

The very next night as I lay in bed I felt a rush of energy come from my ankles, through my legs, up my spine and out through the base of my neck, and there I stood in my front room whilst my physical form was still lying in my bed. I managed to read the time from the carriage clock stood on the brick fireplace before anxiety set in and I journeyed back into my body as quickly as I had left it. I was to experience this once more at a later date and travel further before the fear factor set in, but it did give me definitive proof that I existed beyond the physical form.

Very early in the New Year the phone rang and it was Karen...

"Hello Derek, I just thought you'd like to know I'm pregnant and the doctors have told me it is nothing to do with the IVF treatment but a natural conception."

Jasmine was born in September of 1992.

I was also getting proof from another source. A group of five of us from the Thursday night circle, including Pat, Elen and I, paid £7 each plus our train fare to go and see a lady at the SAGB (Spiritualist Association of Great Britain) in Belgrave Square, London. Her name was Coral Polge and she was considered to be the world's greatest psychic artist. The appointment was an hour and a quarter and in that time all five of us would get a picture that was of a quality that needed to be framed. Many people would want a picture of a loved one that had passed but I wanted a picture of my guide, Grey Bear. When it was my turn she called me to sit next to her and as she began to draw she said…

"This is a man from long ago called an Essene and he is a man of very few words, but he tells me that he has spoken to you twice at very significant times and is pleased that you have taken what he has said seriously and acted accordingly".

During a quiet moment at home I was given the name Habude and his picture now hangs proudly in my work room. I have spelt this name as it sounds but obviously have no idea if this is correct. He was the first of many pictures which include my grandmother, my uncle Bill in his naval uniform and many other helpers from the spirit realms, but I was to have to wait some time before my guide was drawn. On a later occasion Les and Andy were due to come, but on the day Lesley was in hospital for an operation so she gave me her wedding ring, and a ring belonging to Andy that had been passed down through the male side of his family, always via the eldest son, in the hope that Coral would still be able to link in and draw pictures for them. Les had a picture of a young girl who she couldn't recognise, and Andy's was an elderly gentleman with a very wrinkled neck who he couldn't recognise either, but when he showed his mother she produced a photograph of his Grandfather which matched Coral's drawing in every detail apart from a mole on his forehead which Coral had not drawn, perhaps because our defects are not part of our true being but part of our earthly journey. Coral sadly passed on a few years ago.

Chapter Fifteen: Love Arrives At Last

"Your Grandfather's here and tells me his name is..."

It was early March 1992 when John called me into his office to ask me if I would reconsider my stance on overtime. My answer was a firm "No", and this was now as much because my evenings were being taken up with circles and development as it was because of the events that had led to my decision in the first place. In saying no I knew that I would be on the next redundancy list, due out at the end of the month, as I had heard that John had to save one section leader's salary. Due to office refurbishments we had been moved to a temporary area of the shop floor, cordoned off by partition screens, so on the day the redundancies were announced I had to walk the whole length of the manufacturing area, in front of all the workers, and go up a flight of stairs to an office. Inside sat John, with a man from Personnel and the works' welfare officer. The man from Personnel spoke to me...

"Well Derek, this is your three month notification of redundancy and in that three months if there is anything we can do to help you find other employment, we will. You can use the three months to send your CV out to other companies and take paid time off to attend interviews."

"That won't be necessary," I replied.

"Why ever not?" he asked.

"Because you are conveniently making me redundant at the end of June so I'm going to go and sit on the beach for a while and contemplate my future".

He seemed quite taken aback by my answer, but as I got up to leave, with my brown envelope, I could see tears welling up in John's eyes. I turned to him and said...

"Not your fault John, you've only done what you've been forced to. I've enjoyed working with you. You are a good man and a good boss. I only wish there were more like you working here."

I left the office and as I stood at the top of the stairs I saw the shop floor workers all looking up at me so I took a bow and they applauded me all the way back to my seat. The very next day I moved all the work files on my desk to the side and for the next twelve weeks they stayed there untouched. In the mornings I watched as those also given redundancy notices rushed around re-writing their CVs and applying for jobs, but the most amazing thing was that I had no fear or worry about my future. I used the rest of that year's leave up in half days to relieve the boredom.

Brother David, safely returned the previous January from the Gulf, was now stationed in Aldershot, while Peter was busy with many spells working in Gibraltar. Dad had some years earlier been diagnosed as type two diabetic and was learning to manage that, a fate destined to befall all of us in later years except David. Mum, now well into her seventies, tried to go out to the shops each day to keep mobile, but spent most of her time sitting in her chair reading Mills and Boon.

At the church a fledglings evening had been arranged for those of us involved in the platform presentation group. We would all be up on the platform either giving a short talk or two clairvoyant messages. I was to be the first of four of us to do the messages. A few days before this event I bumped into a lady I had sat with in my original circle and as we were chatting she asked...

"Do you have someone in your life yet Derek?"

"I'm afraid not," I replied.

When Neil told me that the girl would find me I had looked at every girl I thought was a possible, but none had made a move and after a while I had given up.

"Right on the edge of your life Derek; very close," she said.

I must admit I dismissed this, as I had come to the conclusion that I wasn't boyfriend material, overweight, soon to be unemployed and nearly 38 years old. The only difference now was that I felt quite comfortable talking with, and being in the company of, women.

On the night of the fledglings evening my turn to stand up and give a message arrived and I nervously got to my feet, stomach churning and I wouldn't like to guess what my heart rate was. I looked over to the far right of the church where a woman was sitting on her own.

"I'd like to speak to you if I may?"

"Yes," she replied.

"Your grandfather's here and tells me his name is John."

"No," was her one word answer.

My first message from a platform and the answer was a very firm no, but I carried on and everything else she said yes to. I left her and did my second message which seemed to go well and then I sat down relieved that my part was done. Two weeks later, I went to the Sunday evening service and when it was over, a lady approached me and said…

"Hello, I'm Frances; I have been searching for you for the past two weeks to tell you my grandfather's name was John."

It was at this point I recognised her from the fledgling's night. She continued…

"When I got home I phoned my sister Bernie in Warrington, because she has a copy of our family tree and I'd realised that I'd only ever known my step-grandfather who was called Jack. When she looked for me, she rang back to tell me that my real grandfather was called John, and because we had been told that that was your first time on the platform I knew it was important to let you know you were right."

"That's very kind of you; thank you."

"Do you do readings?" she asked.

"Yes, but I'm sort of practicing at the moment," I replied.

"That's fine, I'd like to book a time to come and see you."

The evening arrived and she was due at seven o'clock, but seven came and passed as did 7.30pm and I had given up on her and made myself a coffee when the doorbell rang. I opened the door to a rather flushed lady in yellow jogging bottoms and the most vibrant red fluffy cardigan I had ever seen.

"I'm so sorry I'm late, but I've come here straight from the gym in Fareham and I've been driving around for ages trying to find your address."

So she arrived at just after 7.30 and she left about 10.30. After her reading she kept asking questions about how long I had been training and how I had first got involved, and I was more than happy to indulge her interest. The time flew by and as I let her out of the front door, I had the strangest feeling that she wanted to hug me. The following day I had a phone call from Bonita, another of the girls that sat in the circle held at Elen's house and a friend of Frances. She told me Frances, had been really interested in what was said, would like to learn more and would I be interested in meeting her again for another chat? At this time I was willing to talk about my experiences to anyone who would listen, so I said: "Yes." I had only put the phone down for the time it took to make a drink when it rang once again, but this time it was Frances herself...

"Hello Derek, Bonita told me she called and what she said to you, but I want you to know that I don't want to just glean all your knowledge, I think you are a very nice man and wondered if you would like to go for a drink Saturday evening? I can drive over and pick you up or perhaps we could go to a pub near you?"

I was a bit taken aback by this but replied...

"Yes that would be nice, but I am staying at Pat Pitcher's house for a week from Saturday, so you will have to come there."

Pat worked, a couple of times a year, for a week at SAGB and I would house-sit and look after her animals.

Friday arrived, my last day at work. There were to be no formal office farewells as in total 179 were being made redundant throughout the factory. I had collected my P45 and final severance cheque which was the minimum by law that the company had to pay, so no golden handshake, and was saying my goodbyes to the lads when I was told there was a phone call for me. I picked up the handset and it was a manager who had left our site and moved to Stevenage, Hertfordshire to take over a Marconi site there. I had always got on well with this man but was still surprised when he said...

"Derek, I've just been told they're making you redundant, when are you leaving?"

"You've just caught me going out the door," I replied.

"Look, why don't you come here and be my chief estimator? I'll fix up a good moving package for you and I'll pay a good salary. What do you say?"

A move, new job, new and probably better house or flat and a considerable rise in salary, so why then did I reply...

"That's really kind of you but I have things outside of work here that mean a lot to me and I must pursue them, but thank you very much for the offer."

"Ok no problem. If you change your mind in the next couple of weeks give me a call, but after that I'll have to get someone else."

Saturday evening arrives, Pat's front doorbell rings and I open it to a beautifully dressed lady looking completely different to the one that had come to my flat in her exercise gear, and the first thing that went through my mind was what a beautiful radiant smile she had. The pub was only a few hundred yards away and when we got there I asked...

"What would you like to drink Frances?"

"Bitter Lemon please," she said.

We talked all evening and that was the only drink she had and when we left the pub there was still half of it left in the glass, needless to say I had had three pints.

I won't bore you by writing down lengthy dialogue but by the end of that evening she knew I was redundant, and I knew she was an executive secretary at a large insurance company in Portsmouth, lived in Titchfield, about five miles outside of Portsmouth and had two teenage sons Stuart and Andrew. Although she was divorced she still shared the house, a four bedroom detached property on a small estate, with her estranged husband who had been made bankrupt. The house was up for sale because his share from any profits would go to his creditors. I could see how much this upset her because that house had taken them years of hard work to get. After a few more dates I was a little worried as I could tell she was looking for a long term relationship, but I still wasn't sure how I actually felt. The last thing I wanted to do was to hurt her, so I went to Pat and Elen and told them. They looked at each other, then at me, both smiled and that was it. By August I had introduced her to everyone and we were considered a couple. Frances was to later tell me that she had never asked anyone out before and any other time she could not find an address, she would have just gone home and rang to say she was sorry, but she had felt impelled to find my flat. I was also to find out that her idea of exercise was something called toning tables, which involve no real effort as apparently these tables move your limbs for you and you just have to lie there.

More good news was that at circle Les and Andy announced that they were to become parents, with their first child due in March the following year.

Chapter Sixteen: A Time of Firsts

"I wouldn't have made you sing Derek..."

I was in my flat living on practically nothing, Fran was living with her ex-husband and teenage children, far from ideal, but for the first time in my life I felt as if everything was falling into place and that was a great feeling. I had used some of my basic redundancy money to book both of us into a week's spiritual seminar in a Methodist hotel in Hastings, where Pat was going to be one of the workers. I had been on my own the previous year and enjoyed meeting people of like mind all taking their own journey of enlightenment. I had also started training as a voluntary spiritual healer at the Temple, which accounted for my Tuesday afternoons, while Sunday, Monday and Thursday evenings were all taken up with circles. Another first for me was having to compile a CV, and I must say I found this very difficult as I had no real paper qualifications except for my apprenticeship indentures, and I certainly didn't want to go back into electronics as I knew I was bloody useless in that area. Little did I know at that time that my unemployed status was to last for seven years and become the most informative time of my life. I would learn to live with very little and be happy to do so, travel further than I had done in my first 38 years and, most importantly, I was to actually begin to find a purpose to my life.

Within the first few months of meeting Frances she took me to Warrington to meet her sister Bernie and brother-in-law Eddie who both welcomed me with open arms. Fran and Bernie's mother had died some years earlier from Aplastic Anaemia, and their father had very quickly formed another relationship which seemed to consume him so that he had no time for his daughters or grandchildren. He would apparently walk past Bernie in Warrington shopping centre and not even recognise her. It was obvious to me that both girls were very hurt by the situation, so Frances had given up on him and tried hard to dismiss him from her mind. I got to meet Fran's youngest son Stuart very early on in our relationship, but it was to be quite some time before I got to meet Andrew as he told her he wasn't ready to see her with someone other than his father. Stuart and I got on from the moment we met and within a month he was sleeping on my sofa for two weeks whilst he completed an assignment for college in Portsmouth.

Monday trance circle and I am sitting having my hands manoeuvred and mouth opened and closed, when suddenly I am encouraged by a soft Irish accent, through the right hand side of my brain, to say: "Good evening." At this point slight panic sets in and I bring the left hand side of my brain in which tells me I can't do an Irish accent. Immediately my mind is filled with the words to Danny Boy, my mouth is being opened and closed in unison to the words, which makes me laugh and I come back from my trance state with a jolt.

"What's wrong?" asked Elen.

"Nothing, I just couldn't stop myself from laughing," I replied.

As Kevin was no longer with us Pat had taken to sitting after me and her teachers would come through and talk to us. Her guide, White Feather, would never stay long and his messages would be short and straight to the point, but her main communicator never gave a name and said he was happy for us to call him whatever we wished as names were not important, so we called him Mr Green because when he came she would have a green tinge to her face. She took her place in the chair and I assumed one of these two would come, but within two minutes a soft Irish voice said...

"Good evening, my name is Nicolai but please just call me Nick. I wouldn't have made you sing Derek."

"I think you might have," I whispered in wonderment at how this was coming through Pat when I had said nothing about what had happened to me earlier.

"Ok, maybe I would," he said with a mischievous tone to his voice, "but the important message I am trying to get across to you is that, if we are to work together, you can't pick and choose what you will say. If I impress on you to say good evening you must say good evening, the accent doesn't matter, it is the words that matter, because if you change one word you may change the whole context of what I am saying; do you understand?"

I acknowledged this very important point and after a little more friendly banter he left. The next week in circle I spoke for the first time and although the accent was not perfect it did have a soft Irish lilt. Nick still comes to commune with us today.

In November we went to the seminar in Hastings. Lesley had decided to join us and we all had a great week learning about palmistry, numerology, tarot and many other practices. This was Fran and Les's first experience of most of these subjects and they seemed to enjoy every minute, as did I, and it confirmed to me on a very basic level that all things fit together. I decided at that moment that although I found these practices very interesting, if I started digressing to look at them deeply it would take me away from my main focus and I could become a jack of all trades but a master of none. I was also beginning to realise that the main purpose of all this was the progression of me as a spiritual being, and that if I continued on the right path my progress would naturally bring me into contact with those that needed my help. At the end of the week the workers had put together a short play and we all gathered in the conference room to watch it, along with many of the Methodist guests and a few Methodist ministers. Some of the workers took the part of Mediums, and others played their guides and as most of it was ad-lib it was hilarious, especially as our Chinese Face Reader Daphne, had dressed herself up as a nun and was using a toilet brush to bless everybody in sight. I don't know where she got the brush from, and I don't know where the water that was on the brush was from either. What was nice to see was that afterwards everybody was integrated, chatting and laughing together Methodists, Spiritualist, New Age people and the organisers were told they would be welcomed back anytime. I believe the seminar was held for many years after but this was the last time we attended.

During the seminar Frances had received a phone call from her eldest son Andrew who told her that he had decided to leave the bank he was working for as he had been offered a post as a junior purser for a cruise line company sailing out of American ports. He was to leave for Miami to take up his post in three weeks' time. Although pleased for her son, the thought of him being so far away had upset Frances and she couldn't help but shed a few tears.

Later that month Frances got the first offer on her house and there were tears again because there would not be enough left, after the mortgage had been paid-off, for a deposit on a place for her and Stuart, so she turned the offer down. She was now extremely worried that the bank were getting close to the point of repossession, although she was still paying her half of the mortgage. I had a really strong feeling she should have accepted the offer and I sat down and closed my eyes to ask for guidance and once again my thoughts began to flow. I was told that she would receive a new offer in April and that she should accept it even though it would only be five hundred pounds more than the first offer. Then I was left with one other word: 'insurance'. I wasn't sure what the last word was about, when I told Fran she was far from impressed, and at that moment I was pretty sure that if the offer materialised she would turn it down again.

Christmas came and we spent the day at Les and Andy's along with Mum, Dad, Peter and Andy's mum. They had also invited Elen and Pat as they were going to be on their own that year. Dad took to Elen straight away, but not to Pat as she always tried to dominate conversation due to her insecurities going back to childhood. When Frances first met her she had felt the same as my father, but after I had asked her to look beyond this failing to the person within, she had found the same loving caring person I had got to know. I tried to tell Dad this but he was having none of it and was quite vocal in his dislike of her.

The New Year started with yet another first. Andrew was now ensconced on board his Carnival Cruise ship sailing around the British Virgin Islands and I still hadn't met him, Fran's ex-husband had found a new relationship and had left the house and I was invited to do my first service at Cowes Spiritualist Church, on the Isle of Wight, in February. As Pat and Sue were working together it was decided that I would work with Richard and this would be his first service too. I would take the opening and closing prayers and share the clairvoyance whilst he would do the reading and address.

I opened in prayer, which in itself is not easy because prayer is usually a private communication, but I was used to opening and closing in circle so, apart from the fact that 50 or 60 people were sitting below me in the congregation, it wasn't too bad. The healing hymn was next, followed by The Lord's Prayer and then Richard stood up and gave his reading, which was followed by a hymn and then the address. After another hymn it would be my turn to start the messages. Since I had been aware that I would be taking this service, I had been begging spirit to give me a starting point to help calm my nerves. On the Wednesday evening before, I had been shown in my head a gentleman in naval uniform and given the name George and I somehow knew this would be for a lady in the front row. I stood up and my eyes were drawn to an elderly woman and I said...

"May I come to the lady in the front row right here in front of me and tell you that I have the impression of a tall man in naval uniform and I also have the name of George. As this works in thought form for me I won't put the name to the gentleman, but can you take these two things please?"

She looked up at me but didn't speak. I just felt like a right twit and was beginning to panic when the chairperson whispered...

"She is quite deaf Derek."

I leaned over the railing of the platform and asked in a loud voice...

"Can you hear me ok?"

"Not very well," came back the reply.

Instinctively I walked from the platform and moved to the side of her chair and began the message again.

"Oh yes, that is my late husband," she said, and the rest of the service just flowed.

After this Sue decided that she would like to work with her husband and I started to work with Pat, which was to bring a new set of learning processes, because we decided to alternate each week between addresses, which I had never done before, and the clairvoyance which Pat was most comfortable doing. We thought it would help both of us to do the parts we were least comfortable with, but unfortunately for me that was both, so the loo was my last port of call before each service.

On the Wednesday before my first address I was in my usual panic mode and I had no idea as to where I was going to get a reading from, so I sat quietly and a thought was planted in my head which told me to sit down the following day with pad and pencil and a reading would be given to me. When I was ready, I closed my eyes for a few minutes, made my link with spirit and the words began to flow. In ten minutes I had the following piece of verse.

A Child's Spirit Cries

A child' spirit cries, please let me grow
To learn all it is that I need to know,
I chose my earth guardians so nurture me do
But let me be me, not a copy of you.

A child's spirit cries, please let me be free
To experience life for the benefit of me,
Don't suppress me with dogmas embedded in you
I have my god given instinct to guide me through.

A child's spirit cries, let me have my own mind
To help me develop to be one of a kind,
An individual by right is what I want to be
To follow my path to my own destiny.

A child's spirit cries, please let me feel
All emotions of life so that I may be real,
Not false like so many that walk on this earth
Let me always see truth from my moment of birth.

A child's spirit cries, let me find my own goal
Piece together my thoughts to make me a whole,
Let me find success in the way that I choose
Learn to be humble in victory, have grace when I lose.

A child's spirit cries, please just be there for me
So That my spirit of love can progress naturally,
Then you will be proud of a child with a soul
That has both love for itself and love for the whole.

I was to be given many pieces of verse over the following few years, some of which will come into my story. I am well aware that academically they would be considered not very well written, but I will not change them as they were given for a purpose and achieved their aim. After many services copies were requested and I found my dwindling finances getting even smaller as I bought the stamps to post copies to those that had asked for them. Many were later to be sold in a spiritual hotel in Weston-Super-Mare to go towards funding their library. Moreover the poems helped me as an introduction to my addresses over several years, and the sometimes repeated lessons within them were also a part of my learning.

Chapter Seventeen: Moving On

"I came here for charity, I don't want paying...

I was beginning to love Frances in a way I had never known before and she was fast becoming my best friend, my lover, my confidante and support. I was also beginning to understand how vulnerable and lacking in self-confidence she was, and one of the ways this manifested was with her hair. She would backcomb it vigorously to try to give it more volume because she thought it was too fine and if I, or anybody for that matter, mentioned it she would burst into tears. I wanted so much for her to believe in herself and this want was to teach me yet another lesson.

Being unemployed but now working on platforms in churches I mentioned to Pat that I would like to start to give back by beginning my own circle and she thought this was a good idea, although it did mean leaving her Thursday evening one. Within three weeks I had eight enquiries and found that everyone was available on Tuesday afternoons, so I set a date for the first circle and waited for the time to arrive. My sitters were Barry - husband of Jackie who sat in Pat's circle and was training as a psychic artist, three young girls - Debbie, Sarah and Abbey who were all in their twenties, another Carol – slightly older, and two ladies in their late sixties - Vera who was Carol's mum, and Audrey. Initially, there was also Julie – the girl from Havant whose reading I had so badly bodged, but she only sat for a couple of months before work commitments took her away. A few days before the first circle Sarah called at the flat saying she would like a word. After I had made a cuppa she looked at me and said...

"I felt I must come and tell you that Debbie and I are gay, and although we are just friends and not a couple I am not sure whether that makes a difference to us sitting in circle or how you feel about it."

My reply was very brief...

"No difference whatsoever and I feel great, see you both on Tuesday."

After Julie left and following discussions with my group, I then moved the circle to a Thursday evening and asked them whether they would welcome Frances into the fold, because this was now their group and everyone had to agree. They all said that they would love her to come which meant that she could sit if she wanted to. Frances was very pleased but extremely nervous when she joined us the following Thursday. After circle four or maybe five weeks later I noticed that she seemed very quiet and a little upset, so I said...

"Are you ok Fran," and she burst into tears.

I put my arm around her and she buried her head into my chest and sobbed...

"I'm sorry Derek but you treat me differently from everybody else in circle, you seem to expect more from me and when I can't give it, you look so disappointed".

I was quite taken aback as I had no idea I was doing this, so my first instinct was to deny it, but I didn't, I apologised and said I would try not to do it again. When Frances had gone to work the next day I sat quietly and the realisation hit me that she was right, so I phoned Pat and she said...

"Frances shouldn't be sitting with you. She has to go at the right pace for her. I have a place open in my circle now you have left, so ask her if she would like to come and sit with me."

When Fran came round that evening I told her I was wrong and that because I wanted her to go forward so much I was denying her the time to go at her own pace as spirit had given me. I then asked if she would like to go and sit with Pat and she hugged me and said...

"Being in circle is new to me. I get very nervous and in some ways it is an ordeal, whereas you have had wonderful experiences and are now quite comfortable with everything. I want that for me, but I also want to please you and when I can't it hurts me."

"It's not about pleasing me, it is about you being happy with what you are doing," I replied.

The next week she sat with Pat and, for the first time, felt no pressure to perform.

With the circle, voluntary healing and a church service to prepare for nearly every Sunday, I don't know how I was managing to fit in the requirements of the benefits office, but every week I would apply for jobs, send out CVs and make cold calls. All to no avail, but I wasn't unhappy about the lack of response. Most Sundays we would be in a different church in the south of England and then be booked for the following two years in advance. Frances, along with Lesley and Andy, would take turns to drive Pat and I to our venues because neither of us drove. On the odd occasion we would go by train or, if we were serving one of the three churches on the Isle of Wight, we would get the catamaran and somebody would pick us up at the ferry port. The strange thing is we both thought that the hardest place to work was in the Temple where we had both started, probably because we both felt pressure to perform. Now where have I heard that before?

In March Les gave birth to a baby boy, named him Joshua, and the experience of parenthood began for her and Andy. One month later Frances received her second offer on the house for £500 more than the first, just as spirit had said she would, and to my surprise she accepted it, saying that she trusted me and my link to spirit, but as far as insurances were concerned the receivers had taken everything. When I went to bed that night one word was again dropped into my head, 'endowment,' and I then knew what to do, providing, of course, that they did have an endowment mortgage. That evening I asked Frances…

"What type of mortgage do you have babes?"

"Endowment, we carried it on from our first house," came back the reply.

"Bingo."

From the surrendering of the endowment policy, Frances found that she would have enough for a deposit on a place for her and Stuart, so our next job was to find that place.

For my birthday that year Frances had booked me a flying lesson at Goodwood Airfield although she knew I was scared of heights. I had never flown before but she was determined that we would be travelling in the future. When I climbed into the small two-seater aircraft my stomach was churning and the instructor said he had never seen anyone strap themselves in to their seat harness so tightly. We taxied past Frances, who was standing on the balcony of the airfield cafe', onto the runway. I thought I was going to be sick but within a minute we were up in the air and I loved it. The only bit I felt uneasy about was when we turned and I was looking straight down the wing to the earth below, but I must say I thoroughly enjoyed my half hour lesson.

I was still being hassled for money from the freeholders to the flat. I had been paying the ground rent and the amount stated on the leasehold document, £200 a year for maintenance, but they had been billing me extra each year for things such as cleaning the communal hallway, fixing the roof, tending the small piece of earth at the front of the property and many other made-up charges. The communal hallway was cleaned by me as there were no power points in the hallway and I was the only one with an extension lead, and as the garden was a part of my flat, I had been looking after that as it was my responsibility. I had been to see them once and argued my case, to no avail as the demands for money came every year. They were a husband and wife team who owned several freeholds in the Portsmouth area and to be honest it was beginning to get right up my nose, when suddenly it all got sorted in a strange way.

Pat and I had been asked along with two other Mediums to do a charitable demonstration at a local Arts Centre in aid of the NSPCC and we had readily offered to do so. There were probably between two to three hundred people there and we were to do half an hour each. The evening went well and as we were having a coffee after the demo, a lady with the charity logo on her clothes came round with envelopes for each of us. When she came to me she said...

"Thank you Mr Moore, this is a small amount in payment."

"I came here for charity, I don't want paying, please put it back into the fund."

She looked at me and then said...

"Do you know who I am Mr Moore?"

I replied..."your face looks familiar, but no I can't place you; sorry."

"I'm your freeholder, thank you for giving up your time to do this for us."

She then walked away and even though I was to have that flat for another nine years, I never received any demands for money again, and when I sold the place my solicitor was told that no back payments were due.

Frances was due to leave her home in Titchfield and we had only just found her a new place to live, so she arranged with the mother of one of Stu's friends for him to stay with them and she came to live with me, for what turned out to be about eight weeks, until they were able to move-in. Karen and Chris had come to the rescue and were able to store all of her furniture in Chris's parents' barn, which was dry and secure. Chris had his own landscape gardening business and so bought his truck down and did the removals for her. Fran's black Labrador Tammy was put into kennels which really was the only expense Frances had to pay apart from Stu's keep.

Fran's new home was a maisonette in a block of council flats, some now privately owned and some still rented by the council. The flats were only two stories, one maisonette on top of another, so I suppose that equates to four levels in total and hers was at the top of the building. It was not in the best of areas and her block stood next to a concrete high rise of seventeen floors, but the maisonette itself was a very nice, well looked after property and Frances loved it from the moment she saw it. The previous owners were a builder and his wife who had brought up their four children there. The lady told us she couldn't stop her husband from working on it and that she had to put her foot down at night time because he would always find something he thought he could improve. There was a small hallway with stairs going to the four bedrooms, two doubles and two singles, though you could have squeezed double beds in both singles if you had wanted. The master bedroom was huge and would have taken three double beds with room to spare. It also had a walk in cupboard for storage. The bathroom was adequate and the toilet was separate. Downstairs was a fair size kitchen and just the one large living room. Everywhere was nicely decorated and he had knocked a few holes here and there to give the place some character.

On the weekend that Frances and Stuart moved into their new home I was away in Swindon, taking a workshop on the Saturday and the service on the Sunday. By the time I got off the train late on the Sunday evening they were not only in the place, but they had unpacked all the boxes and everything was where she wanted it to be. Once again Chris and Karen had been a tremendous help and some of Stuart's friends had helped Chris carry all the furniture up two flights of stairs whilst Karen and Frances had sorted the smaller boxes and kept the lads supplied with drinks and food. Frances could now start to rebuild her life and at last felt secure again.

Circles were going well, trance was moving on and I was feeling real happiness for the first time in my adult life. In trance Nick had expanded on an earlier lesson when he said through me...

"Remember that life is all about the purpose and motive you have for the actions you take. Doing a good deed is not spiritual if the real reason you do it is for gain or there is a false motive for your action. Giving to someone blindly is not always best so you must consider your actions carefully as you may be prolonging the pain of another if your actions are interfering with their lesson."

At this stage we had moved the trance circle to Jackie and Barry's house as they had a room that could be dedicated to it. Their house was only a couple of minutes' walk from my flat. Jackie, Elen and Lesley were now also sitting for development and were being used for rescue work. Those that had passed over and were lost would be guided to the circle and speak to us through one of the three girls and either Pat or I would take them on to where they should be. For the first couple of times we would ask for some sort of proof which we could check, but very early on we realised that the most important thing was to help those who were lost make their transition as quickly as we could as many were in a state of distress. We were also being called upon to facilitate in house clearances and over the coming years we were called out to many homes in the Portsmouth and surrounding area. I know in this period we helped many people, but judging which cases were genuine and which were not was an important part of our development as some people had their own motives, trying to get moved to a new council house being just one example. At other times we would find someone had mental health problems and imagination had taken over, so we would have to speak to a relative and suggest that perhaps medical help was needed. Rescue work is still an important part of the circle I sit in today, but I know how implausible this may sound to most people so it will only be mentioned once more, in a relevant part of the story.

Chapter Eighteen: The Brighton Line

"Would you like me to add a few more metal studs...?

It was a bright sunny morning in September and in between all the hassle of looking for Fran's new home and actually finding it, we had decided to have a day wandering the famous lanes in Brighton. We had been together over a year and although we weren't officially living together, we were in each other's company most of the time. We had decided to take the train so that Fran didn't have to drive, and as we sat in the carriage she reached for her handbag to find her extra strong mints, which she was a little addicted to, not unlike my mother. She gave a sigh as she began to empty the contents of the bag onto the seat beside her.

"This bag is useless; it's too small, I can never find what I want. I need a bigger satchel type bag with larger compartments."

Her mints were practically the last thing she pulled out and after offering one to me, we proceeded to perfume the carriage with the smell of peppermint, and she began forcing everything back into her bag in a hurry as the train was pulling into the station. We made our way out of the station and on taking a left turn I suddenly noticed a large black handbag in a shop window.

"That's what you need Fran," I said, pointing to the bag, completely oblivious to anything else being offered. "Do you like it?"

She seemed to hesitate before saying it was big enough and had a long strap which she liked.

"I'll buy it for you on the way back to the station," I enthused, feeling pleased that I had spotted it.

We wandered the lanes for a couple of hours looking at all the expensive things we couldn't afford to buy, before eventually finding ourselves outside Brighton aquarium. Frances had a thing for aquariums and just liked looking at fish. I preferred mine smothered in batter with lots of salt and vinegar. In our years together we were to visit many fish houses, including those in Sydney harbour and Miami sea life centre. It got to the point where I would find a nice coffee house and leave her to gaze at her leisure. After the excitement of the sharks, rays and other assorted sea life, we found a little cafe and went in for some lunch. As we were eating and chatting I noticed that she was pushing food around her plate, picking up small pieces on her fork and almost forcing herself to eat them. I must say I had never noticed this before but then we had seldom been out to eat because of the financial situation.

"Fran what are you doing, have you had enough?"

She looked at me with what seemed like a trace of fear in her eyes.

"Yes I have," she whispered.

"Well, leave what you don't want, don't force it down."

"Oh, my ex would always get angry if I left anything. He would delight in telling me he had been all over the world and seen starving people who would fight for my scraps."

"The food on your plate is yours, you eat what you want and you leave what you don't want," I replied.

She seemed a little surprised by this but pushed her plate to one side whilst I continued to devour what was left on mine.

It was time to return home so I paid the cafe bill and we began to walk back through the lanes towards the station. For some reason unknown to me at the time, she kept trying to go back a different way but I was having none of it and managed to get us back to the shop where I had seen the bag and literally dragged her in.

"I'd like the large black handbag in the window please," I said to the man behind the counter.

He was a portly gentleman, about 45 years of age I would guess and I thought to myself he mustn't have grown out of his punk stage, as he had a Mohican hairstyle and several piercings, some attached by small chains. His partner followed the same style but seemed quite a bit younger.

"Would you like me to add a few more metal studs to strengthen it?" he asked. "It won't cost you any extra."

"That would be great," I replied.

I paid the man and we left and made our way to the station to catch the train back to Portsmouth. When we got home I presented the bag to her.

"Thank you very much, but I can't use it."

"Why, what's wrong with it?" I exclaimed.

"Did you not see all the teddy bears in chains and handcuffs in the window Derek, it was a bondage shop. If I take that bag out, everyone will think I'm into allsorts, especially with all those metal studs you had put on it."

To be perfectly honest I had only had eyes for the bag and hadn't noticed anything else in the window. I'm not known for being the most observant of people.

"You'd best put it away somewhere till you're ready to use it," I said.

"You're not angry?" she asked.

"Not at all," I replied smiling.

The bag went into the bottom of my wardrobe, still in the brown paper it was wrapped in.

Fast forward two years, I had a bit of good fortune on my usual Saturday afternoon flutter and won about £200 for a very small stake. Frances loved her bingo so I said we would go out for a Pizza on Sunday evening, as I had no service, and then I would take her to bingo. We played the first half without winning, as usual, and during the 15 minute break Fran asked me if I would like an extra strong mint. She lifted up her bag and began to look for them. It was the bag from the bondage shop.

"How long have you been using that?" I asked

"About a month now, I was wondering when you would notice," she replied.

"Why now?"

"Because I have finally had my ears pierced and realised that what others think of me isn't important, it's what I know about myself that matters. I like my bag."

I smiled inwardly as well as outwardly as the bingo caller started the second half;

"Your first number, five and nine the ………."

Now all I had to do was introduce her to the handcuffs!!

Joke, joke, the last sentence is a joke, and I will admit that the bingo caller did not start with five and nine, but the rest is true.

Frances was now ready to take a big step regarding her hair. Pat had talked to her hairdresser, Karen, and she had agreed to speak to Fran and let her know what she felt could be done. After the consultation, Fran agreed to let Karen cut and colour it and this became a regular event. Each time she went Karen would cut it a little bit shorter and each time Fran would say how much better it was and how much easier it was to manage. This may sound trivial, but believe me when I say that to Fran, it was huge. I am sure there are many ladies that will understand this.

HABUDE

WHITE FEATHER

GOLDEN EAGLE

TWO RIVERS

NICHOLAI

JOSEPH (Andy's grandfather)

Chapter Nineteen: The Eagle Arrives

I got up to answer the door, feeling devastated, had I been fooling myself...

I must now fill in the two year gap between the bag's hibernation in my wardrobe and its resurrection.

I had been offered the chance to work in Germany at the beginning of 1994 and had travelled out with Pat, to Cologne, to meet a lady called Isabel. After spending a night at her house we boarded a train for a six hour journey to a small town called Salzgitter (Bad), and on arriving met a lady called Cornelia Korner and her family. Conny, which is the name she prefers, was a business woman who designed and built houses for well off clients, but as a sideline she rented shop premises in which she sold many 'new age' items such as crystals, Indian headdresses and moccasins. This shop had a large back room where workshops could be held and Pat and I were to do one workshop each and a few readings working through interpreters as neither of us spoke any German. This first trip to Salzgitter opened the door to many more, and Conny and her husband Werner were to become good friends, but unfortunately Isabel and I were never to meet again. During the workshops we were often granted spontaneous rounds of applause which I had a problem with although Pat seemed to take it in her stride. When I returned to England this began to play on my mind and so I wrote to both ladies to explain that I wasn't an entertainer, and my reasons for going were to help those that attended to go forward spiritually. Isabel took offence and I received a very dark letter, written in black capitals, telling me that I should be more grateful that she had offered me the chance to work for her and that she would not be offering again. From Conny I had the complete opposite response. She wrote saying she fully understood and would I be interested in going over twice a year to teach them how to set up their own circles, so that they didn't have to pay for Mediums who were just there for the money. I could fly to Hanover and she would pick me up from the airport, and so began a dear friendship which endures to this day, although Werner has sadly passed through stomach cancer.

When I returned from this first trip, Frances told me her boss David was going back to his native Australia with his family, and she had decided to apply for the position of secretary to the chief executive officer, which was being advertised at that time. David and his wife Pam had become good friends to Frances and had supported her through her marriage breakdown. They had come to England a few years earlier and Fran had told me how he had breezed into the office like a breath of fresh air and claimed her for his secretary. She had done her best to help his wife Pam and their three children Mark, Scott and Tanya settle in their new surroundings, and had also helped Pam find schools for the children. Frances was sad when they left and unsure what the future held for her as she wasn't confident that she would get the new position, and even if she did whether she would be happy.

Pat and I were beginning to get very busy as the bookings were coming thick and fast. We had services booked for about forty five Sundays of the year and the same for the following two years, along with mid-week demonstration and question and answer evenings. The good thing about working as a pair was that if one of us was ill, or been offered work abroad, we never had to let anyone down as we were both quite capable of working on our own.

Frances needn't have worried as she was offered the new position and her future looked secure. I however, was about to have a crisis of my own, although happily it was resolved very quickly. I was sitting waiting for people to arrive for my Thursday evening circle and had closed my eyes to relax and get myself ready, when suddenly my hands were lifted and my mouth opened and I thought to myself: Can I take control of this? I closed my mouth and put my hands down without any problem. My heart sank into the pit of my stomach just as the doorbell rang. I got up to answer the door, feeling devastated, had I been fooling myself for the last two and a half years, was it me lifting my hands and opening my mouth?

Everyone arrived and somehow I got through circle and the short social time afterwards. When all had gone, I took myself off to bed and lay on my back with my hands outside the covers, feeling despondent. Within a few minutes my hands began to rise from the covers and my mouth began to open, so I closed my mouth, put my hands down and pushed them firmly into the covers and held my mouth shut tight. The energy lifted my hands up and forced my mouth open and I then shut my mouth even tighter and slammed my hands back down, but when the third surge came I was left with both hands and arms fully extended pointing to the ceiling, my mouth wide open and this time I could not replace my hands or shut my mouth. I was held there thinking: "If anybody saw me now I would look a right twit." As the energy holding me began to recede, my guide said inside my head…

"Yes Derek, we can lift your hands and open your mouth and yes you can replace your hands and close your mouth, but we do have the ability to hold you there. However, that would achieve nothing and be a total waste of energy. This is a partnership, you trust us and we trust you, and that is the only way we can work together in truth, so the more we become a part of each other, the easier everything becomes."

More evidence for me was on the way, and some proof for Frances, as one day out of the blue she stated…

"I don't think your guide's name is Grey Bear, I think it's Golden Eagle."

I must admit I dismissed this statement, but a few days later she said it again and so I sent up a thought asking that if this was true, please could I have proof within a week as I did not want to be communicating using the wrong name, although by this time I knew he would answer to any name I chose to call him. At circle that week I sent the group into their meditation and when I brought them back forty minutes later one of the girls said...

"That was strange Derek, as you took us into the silence I saw a Golden Eagle flying towards you and I had the same picture in my head as you brought us back."

Proof number one.

Monday, at the trance circle, Pat places a cassette tape in front of me and says...

"I went to a trance demonstration on Saturday evening and the Medium stood up and came right behind me and said I have a message for the man you work with. It's on the tape so you might like to listen to it later."

The tape had a lot of interference but when I listened I could quite clearly make out...

"Eagle, Eagle, Eagle tell him I was here. Tell him to listen through both ears not just one."

Proof number two.

Up until that point I had always thought that all communication came in through the right side of my head and I always strained as if to listen to that side of my brain. As soon as I heard this message everything got easier because I didn't have to strain anymore.

Some months earlier we had booked as a group to go to see Coral Polge. Frances was so excited and when Coral called her to sit next to her, a picture of a young boy was drawn, but it was the evidence given that was significant. Coral said that this boy had not had long on the earth because he had been born with many defects, hair lip and cleft palate being just two of them. Frances could understand all of this and later explained to me that Bernie and Eddie had lost a son thirteen years previous, who was born with those problems, and only lived for a few hours. The picture drawn was of a young boy of about thirteen and the moment Frances said she could accept a child with those defects Coral rubbed out the hair lip and said he wanted his parents to see him as he was now. Frances was to pass the picture on to Bernie and Eddie who were thrilled to receive it.

"Have I drawn your Indian for you before?" Coral asked me.

"No."

"Well, he's here now and I have to say in all the years I've been doing this I have never had to colour the feathers of a headdress like this. They look like Golden Eagle feathers."

Proved, and Frances did say: "I told you so."

On the way out, Frances asked if we could book to go again in a few months, but just the two of us, because then we would get more than one picture each. I think that although she was pleased for her sister, she had wanted a picture for herself. We managed to book for about six weeks later.

In the meantime all the circles were progressing but in Pat's circle, Enid stated that she had decided to leave after two and half years. She said she had done what she wanted and proved to herself that she could marry her Anglican beliefs with those of spirit, so she thanked everyone and said she would keep in touch. In the trance circle we were being given information relating to climate change and the devastating effects it would have on plant and animal life if mankind did not start to raise his awareness and make adjustments in lifestyle to counteract the causes. We were also told of the great changes that would happen to tidal flow, and the damage that water would cause in years to come. We tried to record the weekly circle on tape and managed to do so with a certain amount of success, but there was always interference on the recordings. We were then asked to take this message out and deliver it in our addresses and I was given another piece of verse to help.

Through the eyes of the eagle

In his flight he gazes down
On hill and valley, wood and town
With wings outstretched the eagle sees
The needless spread of earth's dis-ease
He sees his fellow creatures play
Though some to him are natural prey
Once he's full he feels no need
To search and kill till next he feeds
It seems right to him through nature's law
To take his need and then no more
For without waste he knows indeed
That nature will replenish feed
He studies all the creatures fair
The deer, the fox, the fish, the hare
He notes their ways and knows their health
Depends as his on nature's wealth
Yet as he looks he spies one form
That spreads disease to all earth born
Striving through force to gain all power
Over earthly life of beast and flower
With his eyes of boundless scan
Comes recognition this form is man
Then from his view on thermal shelf
He watches man infect himself
And from great wisdom knows for sure
That man alone must find the cure
The solution that's within all sight
That power is equal to all by right
Unless he abides by nature's law
Unlike the eagle man may fall

It wasn't long before another Indian was to join us. I was asked to do a weekend workshop at a lady's house in Kingston upon Thames, a borough of south east London. During the workshop I told Frances that I had seen an Indian with her and he had braided hair and a headband with one red feather sticking up from the back of it.

"What's his name?" she asked me excitedly.

"That's for you to find out as you're so good at it," I replied with a grin, and then added: "Don't just take this from me, wait until you get more proof. Never just except things, not even if they are from me or Pat, you must always question and ask for your own proof."

We left Kingston on the Monday morning and went straight into London for our booked appointment with Coral and the first picture for Frances was of her Indian with his one red feather. Frances was delighted and when she came home from circle the following Thursday she told me that during her meditation she had been inspired with the name Two Rivers, and that she also had dropped into her head the word sequoia, which we knew was a tall tree from California, but when she researched a bit further she found out that it was also the name of a Cherokee tribe.

This year ended with me meeting Andrew for the first time when he brought his fiancée Alison over from the States to meet his mum. Alison was a principle dancer on board the same cruise liner as Andrew and she was an American girl from Harrisburg, Pennsylvania. It was nice to finally meet him, and he was ready to meet me, but most importantly we got on well, which obviously made my relationship with Frances feel more secure.

Chapter Twenty: Realisation of Power

I hugged her and felt so proud...

I think it was a Wednesday evening, about three weeks into the New Year, I was at Fran's place and had just finished preparing dinner for when she got home from work. I was standing by the security doors to the block, having gone outside for a bit of air, when she walked up the path towards me.

"Hi sweetheart have you had a good day?" I asked

"That depends," she replied.

"Depends on what?" I enquired.

"On whether you think that three months salary is a good offer for me to leave the job," she said.

Well this was a bit of a bombshell, but I couldn't make out if she was happy or sad about it. We went into the building and up to the maisonette, where I put dinner on hold whilst we sat at the table and continued our conversation.

"What's this all about?" I asked.

"I was called to Human Resources this afternoon and told that the CEO and his PA didn't think I fitted into their small group as I didn't join in many of the conversations and seemed to be a bit of an outsider. They then offered me three months salary if I agreed to the termination of my contract."

"What did you say to that?"

"I said I would like to think about it and I would give them my answer in the morning. I also told them that the reason I didn't join in the conversations was because most of them were malicious gossip about others, some of whom I have worked with and think to be decent hard working people. What do you think I should do?"

"Let me think about it over dinner and we'll talk again then."

We had our food and while we were eating it became clear to me what she should do, but she would need courage as it would mean standing her ground. After I had cleared away the dinner things I could see she was waiting for me to say something.

"How do you feel Fran, you don't seem too upset by all this?" I ventured.

"Well, I can't say I really enjoy the job, it's not the same now David has gone, but I'm surprising myself at how calm I am."

"Why don't we wait until nine o'clock and then ring David in Australia and see what he thinks. It will be eight in the morning there and you can catch him before he goes off to work."

So at nine she rang Australia and spoke to David who, although very angry for her, said that she had to realise that this was a big multi-national company, and if they wanted to get rid of her they would find a way of doing so. He said that it would probably be best if she took the deal and that she was still the best secretary that he had ever had and that she was good enough to get any job she wanted. When she told me this, I said...

"You don't really want to be there anymore, and I want you to know how proud I am that you've kept to your principle of not talking about people behind their backs and that you actually told them that. Now do you trust me babes?"

"Ye-es," she said a little warily.

"Good because you are going to need to be strong. Remember that this is what I think you should do, but ultimately you must do what you think is right and I will support whatever you decide. I think you should go in tomorrow, and when they call to speak to you tell them that you want one year's salary to go, otherwise you will be going back to your desk to carry on fulfilling your contract."

"I can't see that happening and I don't know if I have the courage to say that," she said.

The next morning she went off to work and returned about two hours later grinning like a Cheshire cat.

"What happened?" I asked.

"It took all my courage but I did what you said and the Human Resources manager seemed quite surprised. He told me he wasn't sure they could agree to that and asked me to wait in his office. He was gone for about thirty minutes and I was getting nervous, but when he returned he just said ok but he would need the name of my solicitor as it must be done legally. I gave it to him and asked if I could leave. He said yes and that the paperwork would be with my solicitor in a couple of days."

I hugged her and felt so proud because the woman I had first met would not have been able to stand up for herself like that. She then said she had made another decision...

"I have a year's salary, so I'm not going to rush to find another job, I'll start looking in about ten months' time. I won't be getting any benefits, because of the money so nobody can make me. What do you think of that?"

I just smiled; Frances was taking control of her life. Three days later we were at the solicitors where he told her she had to sign a termination contract and agree to its terms, one of which was that she could not make any derogatory comments about the company. After she had signed, he handed her the cheque, but as we left the office I couldn't help myself and as we reached the door I turned and said...

"You know that bit about the derogatory comments?"

"Yes," he replied.

"Well, I haven't signed any contract, have I?"

He smiled and said...

"No Mr Moore, you haven't."

I stated at the beginning of the book that this was not about making those sorts of comments, so I'll leave it there.

Frances seemed like a free spirit and joined me as a trainee healer every Tuesday afternoon at the Temple. She also began an aromatherapy massage course for which I was a willing volunteer for her to practice on. Not long after this I took my first solo trip to Salzgitter and came back with enough to buy Fran her own massage couch, for her birthday on 1st June.

Mid-year and Karen announced that she was pregnant with a due date of March the following year. She had gone back to the I.V.F. treatment in the hope of getting a brother or sister for Jasmine and she and Chris were thrilled that it seemed to have been successful. Les and Andy also announced that their second child was due at the same time.

On July 4th I received my birthday card from Fran. On the front was a picture of dragons and unicorns and in large letters the word imagine.

Under this word it read:

> If you dream it
> You can achieve it
> If you imagine it
> You can become it.

Inside she had written:

Be always as a child, joyful and carefree.
Be always full of faith, trust and certainty
in your journey through life that all will be well with you.
And may I always be by your side
to share your journey with you.

In September, Frances and I went out to Miami for a free cruise which took us to Puerto Rico and the islands of St Thomas and St Croix. This was the first time I had been on holiday abroad and Andrew and Alison looked after us so that we wanted for nothing, but by the last evening we had very little money left and we would have a whole day in Miami before our flight home. We were reconciling ourselves to a day in the hotel reception when the last round of evening bingo was starting on board. We only had twenty dollars left so I said...

"We'll spend ten dollars on a bingo ticket for you and save the other ten for coffees and a bite to eat tomorrow in the hotel."

"No, we will both have a ticket and we can just have a walk around tomorrow. We can take some food from the breakfast table in the morning to see us through the day and there is still plenty of fruit in the cabin we can have," Fran replied.

Andrew had asked the cabin steward to make sure we had fruit in the cabin each day, but with so much to eat at the different bars on board we had hardly touched it "Ok, I'll play as well," I said.

A good decision, I won the last prize of the cruise, $250.

We had a great last day in Miami, at the Sea Life Centre. Yes, more fish.

The spiritual work that year was fairly intense with the circles, services, mid-week demos and the trips to Germany. I was also called upon, by the Temple, one Wednesday afternoon to take their weekly Guild as the Medium they had booked was taken ill. The Guild, held every Wednesday was an hour long meeting where a visiting medium would do a short talk and then give messages. I decided to walk to the church that afternoon so I could ponder on what I should talk about. Suddenly a word dropped into my head, followed by a stream of information based on that one word. When I started to talk at the meeting, all of this information came from me in a calm and measured way and when I had finished talking I said...

"I suppose we'd better do a few messages now."

The chairperson quickly stopped me with: "I'm afraid we've run out of time Derek."

I had been talking for the whole hour, but surprisingly the people there didn't seem to mind too much, in fact many came to me afterwards over coffee and said how much they had enjoyed it and that it was nice to have something different for a change. When I got home I felt impelled to sit down with my pad and pen and write.

Thought, the one consciousness

Thought is the basis of all that you need
For all there is in existence thought was the seed
It creates, it destroys; it is the foundation of life
It brings joy and happiness-it brings pain and strife
Expand this concept and you may find it's true
That thought is indeed the creator of you
Through thought you can stagnate,
Through thought you can change
For thought is unlimited and has no fixed range
Into the ether with energy they're hurled
Trillions of thoughts creating your world
Governing your movements, restricting your sight
Stifling progress as through politics you fight
Killing your animals and destroying your earth
Making it barren for those of new birth
And yet in an instant you can change their use
To bring thoughts of love and peace so profuse
Altering your world, bringing hope to new life
Banning from existence all anger and strife
So contemplate now on the thoughts that you send
And send thoughts of love to help bring wars to an end
Create for yourselves a world free from pain
Like the world of the spirit from whence you came
Learn to use this great power for on your thoughts depend
The progression of life or where life will end
Each step you take forward to the spirit within
Takes the whole forward also in the battle against sin
Then slowly but surely we will all stride ahead
To the spiritual oneness we call the Godhead
Where all live in pure love and bask in the sun
United in harmony, all thinking as one.

This took about ten minutes to write and probably breaks all the rules of punctuation and grammar, but within its text it holds for me one of the greatest lessons of my life on this earth and that is that thought is the most creative power in the universe and I have that power. I am the creator of my life and if I wish to change my life I have to change the way I think, and that in turn will begin to alter the world that I live in, i.e. to change the world, first change myself, because I am the only one I have the right to change. I have the power to think and if I hold this power then so does everyone that exists. I'd given up, or had taken away much of this power during my life, and it was time to start to take it back. I'll leave it to you to take those thoughts on to your own conclusions if you wish to.

The year ended with sadness as we had to take Fran's Labrador Tammy to be put down. Her back legs had gone and she could no longer walk, so Fran asked me to ring the vet and make an appointment. Tammy had been on steroids for over a year and now the medication wasn't working. I sat down before we took her, to try and confirm that we were doing the right thing and asked for a blue light to be shown to me if we were. Nothing happened and as we waited in the vets I began to have doubts, but as the veterinary nurse called us in my eyes were drawn to the fluorescent light in the waiting room and as I looked, it turned bright blue. I have to say here that I was the only one who saw it, but then again, I was the only one to ask.

Chapter Twenty One: Two Births and a Wedding

"You are always telling me to trust Derek and now I think you should trust."

Fran's year without work was coming to an end so she had to go to the social to sign on and begin the same process as me in applying for work. She had enjoyed her long vacation and was very sad to think it was nearly over, but work was not easy to find and she was to spend another three years without employment.

In February 1996 Karen gave birth to her second child, about eight weeks early and her new daughter was taken straight into the premature baby unit at St Mary's hospital in Portsmouth. I don't recall how much she weighed but she was tiny, and there were grave doubts as to whether she would survive. Frances and I spent our time with Karen sitting next to the incubator sending healing thoughts and praying she would make it. Karen had made friends with a girl called Michele who had given birth to triplets, also after IVF treatment, but had sadly lost two of them and the third a little boy called George, was also struggling to survive, so our prayers were also for him. Karen called her child Poppy and I am happy to report that Poppy is now a beautiful young twenty year old. George also survived and Karen and Michele continued their friendship. Lesley gave birth to her second boy on the 28th of March and she and Andy chose the name Dominic for him. Les decided to give up working at the bank, it had become a hard sell environment and she didn't believe in talking people into contracts or loans they couldn't really afford, so she trained to be a childminder. She felt this would be rewarding and give her more time to watch Dominic grow. A couple of weeks before Dominic arrived on the scene Frances and I were at Karen's house, visiting and doting over Poppy, when I had this strange feeling and I said to Karen and Chris...

"I have to tell you that I feel there is one more to come."

"No chance, I'm booked in to be sterilized in June just in case. We've decided that two is enough," Karen stated firmly.

"Sorry, can't take it back. It's a really strong feeling."

"I know your links are good Derek, but even you can't get a sterilized woman pregnant," she laughed.

Pat and I were booked to help open a spiritual hotel in Weston-Super-Mare in the first week of June. The hotel had been bought by a Medium called Elsie who had sat in circle in Weston at the same time as Pat. They had kept in touch and quite often met when they both worked at the SAGB on the same weeks. Elsie had booked a young man called Mark to work with her on the Saturday evening and Pat and I would work on the Sunday evening. The Saturday evening was a great success and I still think to this day that the clairvoyant demonstration was brilliant. The place was full of people who were interested but would never have gone into a Spiritualist church, which is why Elsie had decided to open the hotel with the help and support of her children. The idea was that when the demos finished the bar would be opened and people could stay and chat over a drink. When I got up on the Sunday morning, Elsie's daughter Debbie, said...

"Frances phoned early this morning and asked if you could ring her before midday. She said there was nothing to worry about, but she needed to ask you something."

When I rang she told me that Andrew had called her from Miami and told her that he was getting married in Alison's home town of Harrisburg, Pennsylvania in September, and he would like both of us to be there. We could stay at Alison's parents' house and all we had to find was our air fares, he would sort out the rest.

"That's great Fran, but we are unemployed and I don't think we can afford for me to go. I am earning a small amount here and I have a trip to Germany coming up next week, so when Andrew rings back tell him that you will be at his wedding. Unfortunately I won't be able to make it."

Silence on the other end of the phone.

"Are you ok Fran?"

"No not really," she replied.

"Why?"

"You are always telling me to trust and now I think you should trust," she said, and I could hear the annoyance in her voice.

I paused and thought to myself: "She's right, I am always telling her to trust and now I should take note of my own advice."

"You're right Fran. Tell him we will both be delighted to be there and ask him which airport we need to get to. Then ring a few airlines and ask for prices of flights. We'll talk about the rest when I get back."

On Sunday morning, a lady Shirley, who owned a hotel close by and had been at the previous evening came to me and said...

"When I got home last night I felt impressed to draw this picture of a gentleman, and I know it is for you. All I can tell you is, he is Irish and told me that you will recognise him."

I certainly did.

The evening demonstration went ok but, I think both Pat and I were wondering how were we going to follow the previous night and because of this it didn't seem to flow as it usually did. When I got home Frances told me that we had to get flights to JFK airport in New York and Andrew would arrange for a Limousine service to pick us up and take us to Harrisburg, which would take about five hours. She had rung a few airlines and for the appropriate dates we were looking at about £440 each for flights, but I knew this would not be all that was required because, although my suit would probably suffice, Frances was going to want a nice new wedding outfit. With the proceeds from Weston and my trip to Germany we had enough for one flight and Fran's outfit, and to be honest, I had no idea where my ticket was coming from. I knew we would have to book fairly soon because September was still holiday season and she would be devastated if we couldn't get flights. A week after returning from Germany we were both at the Tuesday afternoon healing and as I walked from the healing room, having just finished with a client, the healing leader stopped me and said...

"I don't know why I'm saying this, but I have to tell you that you will go to America."

She then went about her business as usual.

That evening the phone rang and I picked it up to be greeted with the words...
"Derek, you're a bastard!"

"Hi Karen, what's up?"

"What's up? I'm bloody pregnant, that's what's up. We risked it once, just once and now I'm pregnant and I'm supposed to be sterilized next week."

"Not my fault girl, you should have resisted temptation," I said laughing down the receiver.
The following day I was due to take the Guild in the afternoon, so early in the morning I went into town to do a bit

of food shopping for the evening meal. When I left the till I looked at what loose change I had and decided I would risk £2.20 on the horses, so I popped into Ladbrokes, picked four horses and placed a 20p Yankee bet. I went off to the Guild, then back to Fran's for dinner, and as we sat down to watch television I remembered the bet and went onto teletext to check the results. All four horses had won. I can't remember all of the prices but, there was a ten to one winner and an eight to one winner, when I went to pick up my winnings we had enough for my flight and nearly £300 to put away for spending money.

I still visited my parents at least once a week and noticed how fragile my mother was becoming and that her mind was not what it used to be. She was showing the first signs of dementia and my father was having great trouble getting her to eat. She was living on milky coffee and cakes called Rum Babas, although he did say she was eating a Sunday roast and he had worked out that if he put two of everything on her plate, she would at least eat one.

Realisation was beginning to tell me that I was not a Spiritualist, all religion just seemed a way to control the thoughts and progress of people, and although I had no doubt that there were good and genuine people that really believed the preaching of the faith they had chosen, it just wasn't for me. I suspected that for many, in Spiritualism, the pinnacle was to stand on a platform and give messages, while for others just getting a message was enough. I had also learnt that I could not prove life after death, just give evidence that this might be the case. During the previous ten years I had received many messages, some very vague and a few that were right on the money, but did they prove to me that life was eternal? Not really, although they were an integral part of my development because they helped stimulate my interest and instil a need in me to search for more. It was my willingness to go beyond these messages, to go through the pain of soul searching, cleansing and accepting change, that had opened the path to my experiences and my certainty of eternal life. My father never agreed with what I did, but I find it hard to believe that, if he had had the same experiences as me, he would not have done the same. I remember my uncle Dave coming back from South Africa after Aunt June had passed away and he visited Dad whilst I was doing my weekly duty mowing the lawn. During the conversation he told Dad that, before she had passed, June had got involved in a local church in South Africa and that he had not been the slightest bit interested, but on one occasion had gone to pick her up after a Sunday service. She was late coming out as she was talking to the minister so he had gone and sat at the back of the church to wait for her. He said he had closed his eyes, for just a minute, and a voice outside of his ear suddenly said...

"I want you as well my son."

My dad smiled and asked what he had done about it and he said it had brought him into the church and now she was gone it had given him a new purpose and a great belief that she was still with him. At the time this made me both happy for Uncle Dave but sad for me because my father had never asked me about why I had followed the path I had. Any attempt to talk about it was quickly curtailed and the conversation expertly switched to his religion. What it did teach me, however, is that each of us live our life through our own individual experiences and how important that is. It also taught me that this universe will provide proof in a way to suit each individual and their belief e.g. Spiritualists expect to see Indians, Chinese, Egyptians and others that hold within their cultures the same principles of their religion; others expect to see angels, the virgin mother, saints etc. Another thought provoking truth was that I was and always will be spirit, and that the machine manufactured by the physical love of my parents was just that, a machine which holds me on this plain of existence whilst I experience the life I have chosen. The continuation of this thought process, for me, brings infinite discovery and it is difficult to know how much to share. If I truly believe in the progression of the soul, then I must also believe that this progression is the path of each individual part of the whole, and each individual part must journey the path through many lifetimes alone. Anyway, it is not my place to judge where any individual may be or, indeed, whether I am further down the path or lagging way behind. What I do know, however, is that this machine can become worn and scratched and bloody hurt sometimes, as I was about to find out.

We landed at JFK at about four o'clock one very bright, hot afternoon in September and made our way out of the terminal to where people were lined up awaiting their limos as this is where Andrew had told us to go. Unfortunately Derek had chosen to wear the only pair of jeans he possessed for the journey, and he was beginning to sweat profusely in a certain area of his machine and this area was becoming very sore. We waited and we waited and we waited, until we were the only ones there, and after two hours in the heat I was really suffering. We phoned Andrew and told him we were still waiting for our lift and he in turn phoned the limo company who told him that they had gone to pick us up from inside the terminal, and when we didn't answer the tanoy call they had assumed we weren't there so the limo was now half way back to Harrisburg with their other passengers so couldn't come back to pick us up. To cut a long story short, we had to get a taxi to Penn Station in New York, then a train to Trenton, New Jersey where Andrew and Rod (Alison's dad) collected us for the three hour drive to Harrisburg, arriving there at about four in the morning. Chafed is not a sufficient word to describe the condition of my groin and surrounding bits.

Morning came pretty quickly and after a shower, and plenty of talc for me, we made our way to meet the rest of the family, Alison's sister Boo, brother Brian and mother Sheila. Everyone was very kind but I had the distinct feeling that Sheila was very wary of me and she kept asking questions about mediumship and what I believed in, which I answered as honestly as I could. They were a Catholic family, the wedding was to be held at a large, lavish Catholic church and Frances, as the mother of the groom, was to have a private consultation with the priest, which she was worried about.

"What do I say if he quizzes me about my beliefs?" she asked.

"Just tell the truth," I replied

Frances also had concerns about seeing her ex-husband again, and meeting his new partner Peggy. She was worried for me too as he would definitely drink too much on the stag night and might become aggressive, although Andrew had warned him about doing so. I must say I didn't share those concerns and had told them both that if he got into that state, I would just walk away.

During a conversation with Brian and his friend Max, who were both in mid-twenties I mentioned that I liked horse racing, so on our first evening they took me to the local race track. We travelled in Brian's car, a Firebird, and it was pretty obvious it was a big part of his life. I had a great evening and got on well with the two lads, but got the impression that Max was tee total as he only drank soft drinks. By the time we came to leave, Brian was completely blotto and we had to lay him down in the back of the car, where he promptly fell asleep.

"Now you know why I haven't had a drink," Max said. "He gets in this state every time we go out."

When we arrived back at the house Max said...

"Just leave him there, he'll wake up in the morning and make his own way into the house."

So we just left him asleep on the back seat, made our way into the house, and nobody asked where Brian was.

I got to talk to Max quite often whilst we were there. He is certainly one of the nicest young men I have ever met.

The next day, the rest of the party from England arrived including Fran's ex-husband and new partner Peggy. I am not sure if they were married at the time, but the first thing Frances did was to introduce herself to Peggy and then they hugged. Her ex and I shook hands, then Peggy gave me a hug and there seemed to be no animosity from him whatsoever. Bernie and Eddie also arrived so Fran's worries subsided as she had plenty of support if needed. That afternoon, whilst the women were busy making the table decorations, Rod took me out for nine holes on the local golf course whilst all the young people explored the basement, which he had turned into an English pub; beer on draught, dartboard and pool table. All of Andrew's friends would be sleeping on the floor in the basement, but with all the beer and facilities, I'm not sure much sleeping went on. The next day, Frances met the priest at the church and when she came back I asked...

"How did it go?"

"He asked me if I was a practicing Catholic and if I had brought Andrew up in that faith. I told him that, although I was brought up in a Catholic household, I didn't have that faith anymore but that didn't mean I didn't believe in god. I then told him that I had attended a Spiritualist church, was more drawn to their philosophy, and that my partner was a working Medium. He nearly fell of his chair. Then he kept asking me if I would make sure that Andrew kept his vows, treated Alison well and didn't drink too much."

"What did you say to that?"

"I said that Andrew was a grown man, that I sincerely hoped he would do all of those things, but that was ultimately his responsibility."

At the pre-wedding dinner that evening the priest made his way over to our table and sat down with us to eat his meal. We chatted and at the end of the evening he shook our hands warmly and wished us well.

On the stag night, Fran's ex thanked me for looking after Tammy and we had a good laugh in a place called Fantasy's, where Stu's eyes were popping out of their sockets. I'll leave you to guess what sort of establishment Fantasy's was. From there we went to a large hotel bar, where he did have too much to drink and attached himself to poor Eddie, to unburden his soul, and I was left alone.

The wedding went well and Andrew and Alison had about four days before they went off to the Grand Canyon for their honeymoon. In those four days we visited Washington D.C. to see the Lincoln Memorial and Smithsonian Museum. We also went to an Amish community which was very interesting. After seeing the Newly Weds off on their honeymoon, we returned to New York and flew back home, happy. This happiness was curtailed somewhat when I found out that while we were away, Pat had accepted an invitation for us to do a trance demonstration. It was on a Friday evening, for a meditation group that sat each week in a lady's house out in the country, at a place called Swanmore, about ten miles north east of Portsmouth, with a workshop to follow the next day. I wasn't worried about the workshop, by now I was quite confident, but the trance was a completely different kettle of fish. The booking was for the end of January, so there were a couple of months to build up the nerves. I thought: "If Nick comes it won't be too bad and at least Pat will be there so we can support each other." How wrong I was.

Chapter Twenty Two: The First Battle

Within a week we were at St Bart's hospital and we soon found ourselves in the eye oncology department...

The year began with Stuart leaving home to move in with four of his friends, and Fran saying that every now and then she would get a white light flash across her left eye. We put this down to her development, as Carol had had a similar experience with coloured lights during her first phase of development.

Rosie arrived in January, much to the delight of Karen and Chris, who now had three beautiful daughters. Poppy had grown much stronger and although she still had signs of her struggle for life, had a very distinct, determined personality. Karen and Chris, Les and Andy, Kay and Gary were to become firm friends and, although Kay and Gary are now divorced, all the children grew up together like a large family of brothers and sisters. At the present time they are all scattered in different locations, but the bond between them is still there today.

Two weeks after Rosie's grand entrance into the world, was the day of the trance demo and the flush in my bathroom was being severely overused. Frances who was going to drive us to the venue was doing her best to calm me down, but I was pacing the floor, waiting for the time to leave to pick up Pat. About five minutes before we were due to leave the phone rang and Fran answered it.

"Oh ok, I hope you're better by tomorrow."

She put the phone down and looked at me with a wicked grin on her face.

"Pat's not well. She's having dizzy spells and feeling nauseous, so she won't be coming. She hopes it all goes well and is sure she will be better for the workshop tomorrow."

"She's feeling sick and hopes it all goes well!" I exclaimed.

I had felt nervous when I had first sat in circle, when I stood on the platform for the first time and at my first workshop, but I had never felt sheer terror before. Frances could see it in my face and she came over and threw her arms around me...

"Calm down sweetheart, it'll be fine. You've put in hours of work and you knew this day would come. Have spirit ever let you down?"

One more quick trip to the loo and we were on our way. When we arrived we were greeted warmly and the lady introduced herself as Phyllis. The group was about 12 strong, mostly women but there were a couple of young men, and as we sat and conversed I began to feel much calmer. They explained that they met each week, to meditate to heal the earth, and were all very worried about climate change and the damage we humans were doing to the planet. They had arranged the seating so they could all see the trance chair and I took my place, closed my eyes and then handed myself over to spirit. Within a couple of minutes, a feeling of total peace came over me and it seemed to be over in an instant, although I had been speaking for 45 minutes. The communicator had given his name as John and afterwards several of the group described seeing the same gentleman masking my face and they all said he had a beard. At the following day's workshop, which I again did alone as Pat was still unwell, I took along a picture that Jackie had drawn for me, of a gentleman with a beard, and I placed it beside my chair without saying anything. At least three of the group came to me before the workshop started and told me that the picture was of the same gentleman they had seen the previous evening. The workshop went well but I must just relate a short, humorous, if somewhat painful, occurrence.

At the start of the workshop I was taking the group on a guided meditation, with some soft music playing in the background. Phyllis had a beautiful ginger cat which was perched on the arm of her settee next to one of the young men. As they went into the stillness, I could see the cat going off with them. His eyes were beginning to close and his head began to gently nod, as he went deeper and deeper, until he began to slip off the arm of the chair. He suddenly toppled, and as he did, he opened his eyes wide and in desperation flung out his front legs, digging his claws into the arm of the young man sitting next to him, who in turn came back with a jolt and yelled out in pain, making everyone else jump. When they realised what had happened they all laughed, even the young man as he wiped the blood from his scratched forearm. Lesson; never meditate to music next to a sleeping cat.

I was now doing about three or four readings a month, sometimes more, although I never advertised and all of them came via word of mouth. I had made a conscious decision very early on that I wasn't going to use this process to make money, and that those that needed my help would find their way to me. I didn't want to be someone who read cards, or did one reading after another telling people that they would marry a tall dark handsome stranger, live in a big house and have three kids. I wanted to help people to help themselves, and I noticed that most of the people drawn to me, were suffering in ways that I could understand from my own experiences loneliness, having no direction or self-worth issues. To try and understand this more, I decided to take a yearlong RSA counselling course to see if the advice I was giving fitted into conventional teaching. The course had started the previous October, was held one day a week during term time, and by the end I had learnt something very interesting. It appeared to me that counselling took people to a point of understanding, but not to a point of forgiveness, and for me, if you don't forgive you still live with whatever it is that troubles you. Truly forgiving sets you free. By forgiveness, I don't mean forgetting, because if you forget you leave yourself open to suffering in the same way again.

The course was run by two approved counsellors, a lady called Jackie and a young man, Neil. At the beginning of the course we all had to introduce ourselves, and when I explained that I was a working Medium, Neil's response was that he didn't believe in an afterlife and only believed what he could see, feel or logically prove, but I was still an alright person. About ten weeks after the start of the course, I was at home with Frances and we had just switched the television off so it must have been between eleven and midnight, when the phone rang. When the phone rings at that time of night all manner of things pass through your mind but this scenario certainly didn't.

"Hi Derek, sorry to phone so late but you're the only person I know that isn't going to laugh at me."

It was Neil and he was at an overnight sleeping station for the homeless in Portsmouth. He did voluntary work there two nights a week, when he would open up a large house and give rooms to homeless people for the night, and then make sure they left in the morning. One bedroom was put aside for the volunteers to use, to take quick naps during the night.

"I was just taking a short nap and awoke with a start to find an elderly lady standing over me wagging her finger and shouting something I couldn't understand. It has really shaken me up and when I told my co-worker, she told me that none of the other volunteers would sleep in that room because they all felt something sinister, so they all just nap in the chair in the kitchen."

"When are you working next?" I asked.

"Thursday, but I don't start till ten in the evening."

"That's ok," I said, "I'll get in touch with my group and some of us will come there on Thursday at 10.30pm."

On the Thursday evening I went to the house with Pat, Lesley and Elen. Neil led us to the room and Pat and I could immediately sense a presence, so we told Neil we would sit in the room and see if we could help. Neil asked if he could sit in with us, and sat on his own near the door, whilst we formed a small circle in the middle of the room. Within five minutes a lady was talking through Lesley and we managed to take her on to where she should be, but significantly, to get to Lesley she had passed through Neil's body and he had been left in no doubt that this was genuine. To his credit at the next counselling group he told everybody what had happened and apologised to me for being so dismissive at the beginning of the course. A month later I was washing up at Fran's when I was aware of a fairly elderly lady talking to me in thought form. She told me that she was Neil's grandmother and that she had passed from stomach cancer. She also said that in a few minutes her grandson was going to phone and ask if he could come and speak to me, and could I please tell him that the experience he had was not to make him change direction, but to help expand his thinking to make him a better counsellor. The phone rang and within half an hour we were sitting on the sofa with a cuppa and Neil began to tell me that he had booked himself into lots of workshops, how he was now interested in North American Indian philosophy and had booked to go to a sweat lodge weekend.

"Slow down Neil," I said. "Now tell me, did one of your grandmothers' pass through stomach cancer and was she a pleasantly plump lady?"

I have developed the habit of describing bigger ladies in spirit as pleasantly plump.

"Yes," he replied.

I then passed on the message which he accepted, but I heard many years later that he had ignored it and gone his own way.

In February, Enid came to see me for a reading and it was great to see her again. She told me she had been amazed by the number of what she called coincidences, that enabled her to pass on the principles she had found when sitting in Pat's circle, and that she was even having deep conversations with her Anglican friends on life after death. When the reading was over, she invited Frances and I to lunch at her house on the Friday and said she had also invited Pat, Elen, Jackie and Barry. When Fran came home, I told her of the invite and then she asked...

"How did the reading go?"

"Fine, but there was very little directly for Enid, it was mostly about her husband and children," I replied.

On the Friday we went to the lunch and had a lovely time, and then we left Enid to pack for her usual trip to France to see her husband for the weekend. That evening I also went travelling, off to Swindon church, to do a Saturday workshop and then the Sunday evening service. The couple who ran Swindon church were called Marg and David and they would put me up for the weekend and treat me as one of the family. This was nice as it involved a big Sunday roast and all their children would turn up with their partners to help devour it. After the Sunday service, they drove me to Bath station where I caught the train back to Portsmouth and arrived home after midnight to find Frances waiting for me. I hadn't even got my coat off before she said...

"Enid's dead."

I was stunned.

"How, what happened?"

"She was hit by a car yesterday whilst on a crossing in France and died instantly. Her daughter rang Pat to tell her this morning. I'm sorry but I don't know any more than that."

I did think back to her reading, and the surprise invitation to lunch, and it did make me wonder.

This was not to be the only shock that year.

The mortgage on my flat was with the Halifax building society. At the beginning of June they announced that they were to become a Public Limited Company and this meant that I was to get a small windfall, about £1,400 if I remember correctly. When the money arrived I said to Frances...

"On Wednesday we'll go to Vision Express and get some new glasses."

The glasses I was wearing were the first pair I had bought when at Marconi and Fran had not changed hers for many years either. Vision Express had an offer of two pairs of glasses for the price of one which I thought was a good deal and I only expected to be paying £200 for the both of us. As we were waiting for our eye tests we began to look for the frames we wanted. I found mine quite quickly and was pleased because they were cheap. Frances picked hers, they had some fancy name I can't now remember, but when I looked at the price I nearly fainted. There was not going to be much of my £1,400 left by the time we left the shop. We were both called in for our eye tests at the same time. I have to say they were very thorough and when my test had finished, I showed the assistant the frames I wanted and she told me the glasses would take about an hour to make. I waited for Frances and after a few minutes one of the assistants came to me and said...

"We've just taken her upstairs to use a machine we have there, she won't be long."

Frances came down looking worried.

"They have found something behind my left eye, and although they can't be sure, they think it might be a tumour. They have made me an appointment in the eye department at QA (Queen Alexander Hospital) this afternoon at three."

At the hospital, they confirmed what the optician had suspected and told us that this type of tumour was very rare and they would refer Frances to St Bartholomew's Hospital in London, where she would get specialist treatment. Within a week we were at St Bart's and soon found ourselves in the Eye Oncology department waiting room. For something that was supposed to be rare, the waiting room was full. There were children with eyes missing waiting to have false eyes fitted, which was both heartbreaking and frightening, and men and women of all ages with the same diagnosis as Fran's. When we eventually got to see the specialist, an Australian doctor, he told us that it was indeed quite a rare condition in Britain but not so in Australia. Many present day Aussies are descendants of fair haired Europeans and although there was no definitive proof, he said the likelihood was that it was caused by the sun. After examining her eye he said...

"Well Mrs Brown, if you are going to have a tumour this is the tumour to get and yours is in the best position to have it. It is too large to laser so we will bring you in and you will have a radioactive plaque sewn behind your left eye, which must stay there for a specific time worked out scientifically. When that time is up, we will remove the plaque and you will be allowed home, but you will have to visit here every three months, for about two years, so we can measure the tumour and make sure it is shrinking. We will give you some drops which your partner can put into your eye three times a day.

You will receive your admission notice in the next two weeks."

He sounded so positive that we left there feeling quite upbeat and made our way to Waterloo station to catch the train back to Portsmouth. Two weeks later, on Friday the 29th of August, we went back to the hospital. Frances was to have the plaque sewn in the following day and it had to stay there for five days, five hours and so many minutes. She had to walk around with a small Geiger counter and, when she went anywhere in the hospital, she had to check that the plaque had not fallen out as if it did they would have to search to find it. Luckily, I had some of the Halifax money left so I said I would come up on the Sunday to visit. I had also put some aside for those expensive frames she had chosen so that, when we knew everything was clear, I could get her new glasses. When I got back to Portsmouth I went to Les and Andy's for dinner and Andy said he would drive me up to the hospital on the Sunday. The following morning Andrew rang me from the States and said he and Alison were flying over on the following Tuesday and they would like to go up to the hospital on Thursday to see his mum. This was ideal because that was the day I expected her to be able to come home. I awoke Sunday morning and over my coffee I watched the events of the early hours of the morning on the television. Diana Princess of Wales had been killed in France. I didn't have much time to gather all of the details, as Andy arrived and we set off on our journey to see Frances, listening to more on the car radio as we drove. Going into London that day was like driving through a ghost town, there were no cars on the road and no people on the streets; it was eerie.

In the hospital all the talk was of the mornings events and the air was full of sadness. Frances had had her op and was sitting by her bed, eye patch over her left eye and trying to read a book with her good one. We stayed for about four hours and after confirming, that if all was well she could leave on the

Thursday, we drove back through the still empty streets of London. Neither Andy nor I have ever forgotten that day.

Andrew and Alison came to pick me up on Thursday and we drove to Richmond where Andrew parked as he didn't want to drive into London. We caught the train in, collected Frances from St Barts and made our way back home. Fran was thrilled to see her son and as he and Alison were over for two weeks they would have plenty of time to spend together. I was booked to take a workshop at Havant church on the Saturday. As it was the day of Diana's funeral I phoned to ask if they wanted to cancel, but was told that they would like to go ahead. Eight people turned up and at eleven o'clock we stopped for five minutes silence, to reflect and say our own private prayer.

When Andrew and Alison had gone to back to their ship I sat down with Frances and said…

"We need to be together all of the time Fran. I don't think we can afford to keep two homes going, so I think we should go to the Social Security office and tell them that we are now living together, but this means we must first put our flats on the market and sell whichever gets the first offer."

To be honest, at this point we were not out of each other's company for very long anyway and were probably breaking a few rules, although we were not claiming any more than we should.

"I think you're right," she said, and the next day both flats were on the market.

Fran's place sold within a week and I could feel her sadness, but financially things were very tight. There was no way we could keep both places and mine was obviously going to take a long time to sell. We moved back into my flat, and sorted out what benefits we were entitled to, as a couple now living together.

Chapter Twenty Three: Holidays to Remember

"I think that's my cousin Chrissie sitting at the front..."

Whilst we were packing to move everything from Fran's maisonette to my flat I came across two insurance documents, for her and her ex-husband, and asked Fran what I should do with them as they looked like paid up policies.

"Just throw them away, the receivers will have cashed them in and taken any benefits to pay off his creditors," she said. "They took everything."

For some reason I didn't throw them away, just packed them up with all the other paperwork. When we were unpacking at my flat, Frances came across them and said...

"I thought you were going to throw these out."

"I was, but if it's ok with you I'd like to phone the insurance company and just check before I do."

"You can if you want to but I'm sure they took everything."

The next day I telephoned, Frances told them that I could speak on her behalf and they said they would check the policy numbers.

"Well Mr Moore these are both paid up policies and if Mr and Mrs Brown send them in, with the signatures of both applicants on each policy, we will be pleased to pay out what is due."

Frances couldn't believe it, but was worried about contacting her ex-husband. She phoned that evening and, to his credit, he couldn't have been nicer.

"Give them to Stuart to bring to me and I'll sign yours, but I'll keep mine and deal with it myself as I'll probably have to let the receivers have it."

Just before we moved back into my flat we had given the car to Stuart as it was beginning to cost us too much and Frances was fed up with driving. Stu took the policies to his dad and we had Fran's back within a week which we promptly posted off to the insurance company.

"How much do you reckon I'll get?" she asked.

"The policy cost was only £10 per month over ten years, so £120 per year for ten years is £1200, plus a bit more for benefits. I reckon about £1400," I replied.

Two weeks later she received a cheque for just over £6,000.

"I'd like to pay a couple of thousand off this mortgage to get us out of negative equity, buy some new clothes as we haven't had any for years and book a nice holiday somewhere tropical if my doctor says that it's ok," she said beaming.

When we went back to St Barts for her next check-up they were very pleased as the tumour had shrunk to about half its original size. I have to say that their reaction to this made me wonder how successful this treatment usually was, as the consultant brought in four of his colleagues to look at her eye. "As long as you wear sunglasses that protect all around the eyes then there is nothing to stop you going on holiday," he said.

When we left the hospital we went straight to a shop and bought a good pair, and within two days we had booked a two week all-inclusive holiday to Sri Lanka. I wrote a letter to the benefits office, explained everything and told them we understood we would not be due any benefit for those two weeks.

The spiritual work was full on and I let Pat know the dates we would be away so that she knew she would be on her own for two Sunday services. I had now been working in this way for nearly five years and, as we served each church twice a year, I was beginning to notice patterns, like who would be sitting in which chair and who wasn't listening to the address, just waiting for a message. Sometimes it was as if they were trying to draw you to them. This was beginning to play on my mind and later would lead to me breaking a lesson taught earlier. I also had a problem with readings because people would come and then try to book again within a short period of time. I would tell them that a reading took them at least a year downstream, and if they came three times I would also remind them that they should not be trying to run their lives by having readings, they had to make their own life decisions. I was beginning to understand why, in some cases, the Spiritualist rule of stopping at the point of proof of survival was not such a bad thing. However, the way it worked for me was that spirit would never tell someone what to do, but always put advice across in such a way that the final choice was the sitters. This was never more apparent than one day when I had a call from a lady I had trained with in my first circle at the Temple.

"Hello Derek, if I send a young couple to you this afternoon would you be able to give them separate readings please. It is rather urgent, but to be quite honest I know too much about a certain situation to be able to do this myself, and I trust you to be honest with them."

I must say I was intrigued by this and agreed to see them. The young lady was in her mid-twenties and very pregnant. He was quite a few years older and when I looked into his eyes, a strange feeling of wariness came over me. I asked him to go into the bedroom and then took her into the living room and began. The significant part of her reading was...

"You can get back what you have lost and keep what is due, but to do this you must be prepared to give something up and walk away."

I didn't really have a clue at that point as to what it all meant, but it was going to become crystal clear. She however smiled and said she understood and had got what she came for. She then swapped places with her partner and spirit said to him...

"You are free now and must choose your direction carefully. If you don't want to repeat the patterns of the past you perhaps should set others free and not try to contain them."

I was now beginning to second guess what I was talking about, and these ideas were confirmed when after his reading he said...

"Do you know what I've done and where I've been?"

"No," I replied

"I was a Category 'A' prisoner," he said and then just stared at me before saying: "What do you think of that?"
I replied: "You didn't come here for me to make a judgement on you and it's not my place to do so; you came here for a spiritual reading and that's what you've had."

They left and I sat down to thank spirit for all that was given and, as I always did, I said I hoped I had not let them down. My thoughts were taken from me and I was told how well I had done and that although it may be right to abhor an act, you should never judge the spirit.

An hour later my friend rang and she said the lady was thrilled because I had told her that she would keep her new child and get the two children that had been taken from her back. She had her two children taken away when she took up with this man, and now she was pregnant by him the authorities had told her that her child would be taken from her the moment it was born. She didn't tell my friend the bit about having to give something up and walk away. This is a great problem with readings in that people only pick from them what they want to hear. I don't know what the outcome was in this particular case.

On a rare Sunday off, Frances and I strolled down to the Temple for the evening service and sat in our usual place at the back and to the side of the main congregation. As the service proceeded I looked ahead down the line of chairs in front of me and I suddenly thought I recognised a lady in the front row. I nudged Frances and whispered...

"I think that's my cousin Chrissie sitting at the front."

After the service she stood up and walked up the aisle and although I hadn't seen her for at least eighteen years she was instantly recognisable. We hugged and I asked...

"What on earth brings you here?"

"Long story," came back the reply.

I introduced her to Frances and then asked...

"Got time to come back home with us for coffee and a catch up?"

We went back to the flat and she began to fill me in with what had happened in her life.

Brief scenario: First marriage breakdown, two children, Pam and Lawrence. I knew these two children until they were about ten and twelve but, when I lost touch with Chrissie, obviously didn't see them again. Second marriage ended in divorce, after two more children Joy and Jenny, when husband decided he would try drugs and kept Chrissie and the children prisoner for a year, before they managed to flee to a refuge in Salisbury. After the divorce husband number two committed suicide. Chrissie was now a prison visitor and was visiting a man convicted of double murder. He was later to be released after serving 18 years and he and Chrissie would marry, with disastrous consequences which would lead to him throwing himself out of a top floor window and committing suicide, but not before Chrissie finding out that everything he had told her for eight years was a lie.

After all of this she still says she would not change one second of her life because she has learnt so much. We are still in touch to this day, every now and then when she comes to visit for a few days, I learn more about her life and she usually has a new chapter of disaster to tell. I've come to know her as an extraordinary woman whose life story would make a remarkable book.

Off to Sri Lanka in March for a marvellous holiday, if not a marvellous flight. I won't dwell on that too much but let's just say I will never fly with that particular airline again. As for Sri Lanka it was beautiful, turtle hatchery, Pinnawalla elephant orphanage, Indian Ocean and friendly humble people.

When we arrived home the benefit cheque was waiting for us. Whether this was because we had been honest and told them we were going or because it was different rules for those on income support I do not know, but the money was welcome.

Later in the year Andrew, who had now risen quickly through the ranks to chief purser, paid for us to go out for a second cruise. He had been transferred onto a ship called The Spirit, now there's a coincidence. The Spirit sailed from Vancouver, up through Alaska, from May to the end of September and then it followed the hump back whales as they made their annual journey from the cold waters of the Arctic to the warm waters of Hawaii. We were to go on its final trip of the year, a seven day cruise from Vancouver to Seward, and then a train to Anchorage from where we would fly home. When we boarded the ship in Vancouver Andrew had managed to get us a cabin with a balcony and also arranged four excursions. When Fran found out about the balcony and excursions she was so excited. Andrew told us that he was given free trips for his parents twice a year, and that the excursions were free as well. How true this was I am not sure because I know from brochures that the excursions alone would have cost us nearly £1000.

We set off from Vancouver and stopped for excursions in Skagway, Ketchikan, Sitka and Juneau. We went to see the Mendenhall Glacier, took a trip on The White Pass & Yukon Railway up through the path of the Klondike Gold Rush, went bear watching on a small island only accessible by sea plane and finally, whale watching. The ship had a casino on board and each evening we would change $20 to quarters and spend an hour on the one armed bandits. Every evening Fran would quickly loose her share and come waltzing over to see how much of mine she could pinch, but at the end of each evening I would have won our money back, plus a little so we would spend the rest of the evening in the Piano bar where the male pianist would play requests. We had arranged the holiday so that when we got to Anchorage we would have a day and a half to explore, but by the end of the seven day cruise we were once again down to our last $40 or so. On the last evening we changed our $20 to quarters and went our separate ways to play our favourite machines. This time it was my turn to lose my money quickly, so I made my way over to see if I could pinch some of Fran's.

"Got any quarters left babes?" I asked.

"I'm down to my last three," she replied.

She put two through the machine and said...

"Last one going in."

She put it in the slot and pulled the handle. It took about five seconds for the reels to stop turning and then the machine went crazy, lights began flashing, a siren blared out and two of the casino staff came running over; she'd only hit the jackpot. I will always remember the way her face lit up with sheer joy and although it was only $250 it was like a million to her as she had never won anything in her life before. The cashiers paid her the money and presented her with a cheap tee-shirt that had pictures of bells and card suits on it and, in big bold letters, the words, **Been There, Won That**. I had no doubt that we were once again being looked after.

When we reached Seward we said goodbye to Andrew and Alison and a train took us on the three hour journey to Anchorage where, with the $250, we were able to explore and eat well before the plane took us back to England. Our photo album is full of pictures of beautiful Alaska and all its wildlife and we agreed that this was the best holiday ever; thank you Andrew.

Chapter Twenty Four: Back to Work

"I can't go on like this Derek, not knowing where the money for bills..."

In early January 1999 I went with Jackie to a hotel in Babbacombe near Torquay to do a demo. I had been there on my own before, but now Pat and I were taking it in turns to get Jackie working as a psychic artist. Her pictures had progressed from little round circles with facial features to very good pictures, and now it was her turn to prove to herself that these images were coming from spirit. The demo was on a Thursday evening and she drew six pictures while I added the clairvoyance that went with the images. This is not an easy way to work as you have to trust that what you are being given, goes with the person being drawn. All six pictures were taken and Jackie was on a high as we returned home. I tried to tell her that it would not always go so well, but my words were falling on deaf ears. Pat and I took her out several times, but unless 100% of the pictures were taken she would go into a deep depression. No matter what we said, it wasn't perfect and perfect is what it had to be. Where have I heard that before, however, whereas I had understood this lesson Jackie was having none of it. After a while it got to the point where we really didn't want to be working with her and she really didn't want to be there.

Whilst we were in Babbacombe, David and Pam who were over from Australia in Portsmouth to catch up with friends, had taken Frances out to lunch. When I got back I asked...

"How did lunch go with David and Pam?"

"It was lovely to see them but they were sorry to have missed you and send their love. David kept on asking me when we were going to get married."

"Oh yeah and what did you say to that?"

"I said I didn't want to get married unless it was under a palm tree somewhere abroad, to which he replied that they have a palm tree in their garden and if we got married there he would pay for the wedding."

I laughed.

My Thursday evening circle had come to a natural end, after nearly six years, and I merged those that were still sitting into Pat's group and we all sat at Elen's house. On our third visit back to St Barts they told Fran that the tumour was gone and that all they could see was scar tissue, so they transferred check-ups back to QA in Portsmouth, on a six monthly basis. We went back to Vision Express and amazingly, found that she had no change to her prescription, so I produced the money I had put aside and she got the frames and glasses she wanted. We felt blessed because it seemed to us that not many, if any with this cancer, come away without some damage to their eye. We only had one appointment at QA before she was signed-off which meant she would be off incapacity benefit and the whole rigmarole of signing-on would begin again. With this playing on her mind she said to me…

"I can't go on like this Derek, not knowing where the money for bills is going to come from. I know we have been looked after, but this waiting until the last moment for things to happen is stressing me out and I know you won't change your principles and start to advertise and make what you do a source of income, so I am going to try harder now to get a job."

"Ok sweetheart but if you go back to work then so must I," I replied.
She was right, I wouldn't change the way I felt as for me it wasn't and never would be about making money. This primarily was about the journey of my soul and helping

others was a bi-product of that journey. Within six weeks Fran had secured a position as secretary to a small firm of accountants and I was awaiting an interview work day at the Inland Revenue. I know, Boo-Boo. The day before Frances's first day at work we received an electricity bill for £139 and, because she had to work a month before she got her first wage packet, we had no way of paying it. I put it on the mantle in the hope that the red demand would not arrive before she had been paid. I have never forgotten the amount because of what happened next. Fran had gone off to her new job and the phone rang…

"Hi Derek, Lesley from the Temple here, I have a couple who have come in asking for readings, do you think you could help me out if I send them up to you?"

"Yes ok when will they be here?" I answered

"About half an hour if that's alright?"

When I opened the door I instantly recognised the man as he worked in the stores at Marconi. I had never spoken to him before, but had often seen him rushing around the shop floor in his brown coat. I also recognised the lady as I had given her healing at the Temple.

"Come in."

"Thank you."

They introduced themselves as a married couple, Nick and Jan. I made them both a drink and then asked…

"Do you want a joint reading or individual ones?"

Jan was quick to answer. "Individual, because whenever we have a joint reading it ends up being all about Nick and I get nothing."

I smiled and then asked Nick to go into the bedroom with his cuppa.

"Before you start," she said, the church told us that you were unemployed and therefore wouldn't take payment, so this is a donation."

She placed a sealed envelope on the coffee table, I said thank you and proceeded with the readings. When they left, I opened the envelope and found £140, so I interrupted Fran's first day with a phone call to tell her what had happened.

"You can't take that Derek," she said. "You'll have to ring Lesley and see if she has a telephone number for them."

I rang Lesley and luckily because they both had healing cards she had their number. I rang and Nick answered...

"Hello."

"Hi Nick, its Derek here. You came to see me this morning."

"Oh yes mate what can I do for you?"

"Well, I think £140 for two readings is a bit much don't you?"

He paused and then said...

"Hang on, I'll put the wife on."

Jan came to the phone and before I could say a word she stated firmly...

"We needed something from you this morning and we got it. I know you need that money so that's our donation."

She then put the phone down on me. I paid the lekkie bill.

I was to meet them again quite soon when they came to Tuesday healing, and as the years went by they became good friends to Frances and I. There will be further mention of them as we move forward with the story.

Just before my workday at the Inland Revenue, Boo-Boo, an application form for an estimator at Marconi was dropped through my door, by either Chris or Dave who both lived nearby. The note with it said there was a position vacant and that as Ken was now chief estimator, any application from me would be looked upon favourably. I knew the salary would have been £18,000 per year plus, whereas the revenue assistant's job I was going for was only £7,500 year. I went to the workday and about a week later was offered the position. After much deliberation, I said to Fran...

"If it's alright with you, I'm going to take the job at the Revenue. I know it's not much money but I feel if I go back to Marconi I'll regret it as it will feel like a backward step."

"That's fine Derek. We will have enough between us to manage and that is all that's required."

I started work in the first week of July almost exactly seven years after being made redundant. It was monotonous as I spent my days putting things into alphabetical order or following the same process on the computer screen hundreds of times a week. After six months I could stand it no longer so I applied to take an internal test for promotion which I passed, and after an interview my job title changed to revenue officer, which meant a £2,500 increase in salary. To be honest, I did not expect to pass because, at the interview I was asked if I had any questions and I replied...

"Yes, will overtime be compulsory and do you expect me to tell lies to people over the telephone."

"No, overtime is voluntary and we expect you to tell only the truth when on the phone."

"Good, because I won't be doing overtime and I won't be telling lies."

I thought I might as well get it out there before anyone assumed differently.

As far as the church work was concerned, Pat and I had been doing more and more as individuals, but came together quite often as some churches liked having the two of us. I still had bookings extending to two years ahead, so life was extremely busy. Pat had acquired a new friend, a black and white cat she called Finlay who had been abandoned and was scavenging on the streets. When he made his way into Pat's house and decided to stay, needless to say Flora was not too happy about the new housemate. Towards the end of the year I could see Fran was becoming very unhappy in her job because, although she got on well with all of the accountants, the main man was a pain in the proverbial and when he gave her just £5 as her Christmas bonus, she came home in tears. I took the £5 and returned it to him with a letter thanking him for his kindness but telling him that we could manage without it. I told Fran that if she wasn't happy she should hand in her one month's notice.

"You don't mind?" she asked.

"We said we would go back to work, not back to misery and unhappiness. Put your notice in and I'm sure you will find something better."

Before the month was up she had secured an executive PA's position with a big company. Her salary was a lot more money and the offices were within walking distance from home. We later found out that the firm of accountants had several secretaries resign due to difficulties with this one man. I won't expand on this as the reasons are to do with religious and cultural differences.

We were now both in full time employment, which eased the pressure financially, and as we settled into our new circumstances it felt as if a new phase of life was beginning.

Chapter Twenty Five: I Am God

I know this statement might be considered controversial, but please bear with me and I'll try to explain...

In the trance circle, Steven arrived. Steven was to be, and still is, my main communicator and in the following years would teach me so much. When he first introduced himself, he said that, although he had lived his previous existence in eastern culture, he had chosen the name Steven because he was talking to those of western culture and anyway he liked the name Steven. When he comes, I feel the gentleness of his manner, his soft quiet speech brings with it such wisdom. He taught me that there is a vast difference between intelligence and wisdom and that even if you don't have great intelligence you can still have great wisdom. Perhaps intelligence without wisdom is not a wise thing to possess. He said he had spent much of his earth life in Chou Pen or Pen Chou, I can't remember which way round it is, and I don't know if I have spelt it correctly, but he said it was in the place we now call Taiwan. He said he had been a teacher of philosophy but not in the way it is taught now. Steven's arrival, and wisdom brought the real meaning to me of a piece of verse I had been given many years before.

I AM

I am from here, I am from there
I am indeed from everywhere
I can be man, beast, flower or tree
I am all being, yet I'm always me
Sometimes in sight, sometimes unseen
I am all that lives where're you've been
All great deeds have been inspired by me
For I am your thoughts and your philosophies
I am religion, I am destiny
To believe in your-self is to believe in me
I am your peace, I am your love
I am the earth you tread and the sky above
I am all direction, I am limitless
I am those you despise, I am those you bless
I am your stars and your eternal space
I am the light that shines from your baby's face
I am all there is, I am all you see
For nothing exists outside of me
You can call me God or the Great Divine
I am always yours as you are mine
For **I AM YOU** and **YOU ARE ME**
Interwoven we form **ETERNITY**
We exist together, can't exist apart
For I am your body, you are my heart
I am all things to you; you are all things to me
So let's exist as one in tranquillity
For if we can all life will be
Peace, Truth, Love, Pure Ecstasy.

This is when I realised that I am God. I know this statement might be considered controversial, but please bear with me and I'll try to explain. I am God but no more so than you and every living thing in existence because, if all come from one source, whatever you wish to call that source, all must be a part of that source and together make up the whole. This brought a whole new meaning to my life because I had to accept, that whatever was happening in this world or indeed any world, I had a responsibility for it, i.e. if a gun is being pointed then I am pointing it and what's more I am pointing it at another part of myself; if a bomb is being dropped then I am dropping it and potentially killing hundreds of parts of me. Conversely, if love and compassion is being shown somewhere then I am showing it to, yes you've guessed it, other parts of me; and so the examples go on and on and on. I now began to understand fully the previous lesson; although it may be right to abhor an act, you should never judge the spirit. It also taught me that perhaps free will is of the spirit, not the material mind. I hope this gives some explanation of my statement and also the title and authorship of this book. There is perhaps much more to be taken from this simple verse, but as I have already stated I believe that each individual part of the whole/me is on its own journey and therefore must find its own path of understanding, and that many parts of me may already be far beyond my point of understanding.

At this point my addresses in churches began to change and I began to look at life and others differently, trying hard not to judge and trying hard to understand when actions troubled me. Please don't get the idea that I turned into some sort of saint as nothing could be further from the truth. I found this hard and still do to this day and, what's more, I have failed miserably on numerous occasions, but I do try and when those failures occur I have learned to forgive myself. My concept of my guide and helpers also changed because now I recognise them as parts of my being, but having built up my love and friendship with them over several years, I have decided to keep them as separate identities.

It was around this time that Jan and Nick asked Frances and I if we would run a small development group in their house and we agreed. We went on alternate weeks as I didn't want Fran to feel that I was interfering in what she was doing and I also wanted her to become confident in her own abilities. She felt more in tune with eastern philosophies and the teachings of the Indian Guru's such as Sai Baba, and would prepare her weeks diligently, whereas my way of working was to link in and trust to the inspiration of my guides. We were to run this group for nearly a year, until Jan's mother was taken ill and they moved her in with them as she needed constant care.

Chapter Twenty Six: Wedding Trip

I glanced at Brian and he was asleep at the wheel...

The New Millennium has just started, I have racked my brain trying to remember where I got the £3,300 pounds from but I can't be sure. I may have changed from an endowment to a repayment mortgage, so it may have been from the surrender value of the endowment policy, but wherever it was from it meant that we could now put my grotty little flat back on the market and look for something better. I shouldn't really denigrate my little home, as it has been my sanctuary and the place where I've had so many wonderful experiences, but it was time to move on and for Frances and I to create a new home together. We often talked of moving to the country and living in a cottage or bungalow with beautiful views and at one time, along with Pat, Elen, Jackie and Barry, Les and Andy, had taken a trip to Wiltshire to see what was available. I think it is fair to say that Frances and I would have taken the risk and just sold up and gone, but Les and Andy said that they had the two boys to think of and were not ready, and the others did not seem totally committed at that time so the idea was put aside. After six months we had only had one viewing on the flat and I turned to Frances and said...

"The only way this flat is going to sell is if someone knocks on the door and asks to buy it. If we have to stay here we may as well use the money to make ourselves more comfortable. What do you think?"

I knew the thought of staying was a blow to her but she said...

"I think you are right, it's not going to sell so why don't we get the bathroom sorted. We can get a few companies to come and give us quotes for a new suite and tiling throughout."

When we got the quotes back I nearly fainted as the cheapest was for over £5,000. Stu came up to visit us a few weeks later and Fran was telling him about the high quotes we'd had when suddenly a thought flashed through my mind and I blurted out...

"Bugger this Fran, get on the phone to Pam and David and ask them if we can go over in September and stay with them for a couple of weeks. The three grand will cover the airfares and leave a bit for spending money. We can't sell and we can't afford a new bathroom so let's bloody well enjoy it."

Her face shone with the broadest of smiles and Stu just started to laugh.

"Are you sure?" she asked.

"Yes, and while you're at it why don't you ask if we can get married while we're there."

She picked up the phone and rang Australia...

"Hello Pam, its Frances."

After a few pleasantries she posed the first question and Pam replied...

"Of course you can come over but I think you'll have trouble getting flights as it will be right at the start of the Olympics."

Oh shit, hadn't thought of that.
Frances continued...

"Well if Derek can get flights we'll ring you back and I have one more thing to ask."

"What's that?"

"If we can get there, can we get married in your back garden?"

A loud booming voice came down the phone from David who was listening in on an extension…

"You bloody beauty Frances, of course you can. Let us know when you have flights and we'll arrange the rest and I'll pay for it as I promised."

"There's your answer," said Pam.

As soon as Fran put the phone down I got onto the airlines and managed to secure flights at about £770 pounds each. We would fly out to Sydney on the 20th of September, with a seven hour stopover in Singapore airport, and the flights back were from Sydney to Melbourne, Melbourne to Singapore and then back to London seventeen days later. Not ideal but hey, we didn't care, we were going to Oz. Fran immediately phoned Pam and she told us that we would have to go to the Australian Embassy to file our wish to marry. No problem for us, but we had only given Pam and David six weeks to organise our wedding. I should have known that most of the rest of the money would have to be spent on wedding rings and outfits, so the credit card was going to take a hammering whilst we were out there.

We went to the embassy in London where, after examining Fran's divorce papers and asking a few questions, they provided us with the paperwork we needed. We booked our leave from work, told our families, bought the rings and before we knew it we were on our way to Singapore. When we arrived twelve hours later we managed to get a room in a hotel in the airport and get five hours kip before continuing on to Sydney, arriving at eight in the morning. Pam and David were there to greet us and as we began the drive to Turramurra, Pam said…

"We're not going to let you sleep because if you do you'll be chasing sleep all the time you are here, so I will be taking you out to see some wildlife today and this evening we'll down a few bottles of wine and then let you rest so you will be fresh in the morning. Tomorrow we have an appointment with the celebrant to sort out the marriage service and I've already warned her that you won't want the traditional wedding vows."

We arrived at the house, had a quick look round and a drink and then Pam took us to a small wildlife park where we purchased a few bags of food and went to feed the kangaroos. As I was feeding them I suddenly looked round and Frances was walking briskly across the field with her two bags of food held out in front of her and two large Emu's running full pelt towards her. When they reached her they pecked all the food and the bags from her hands and her face was a picture of sheer delight. If they had come running towards me at that speed I would have had to change my trousers, but where animals were concerned, Frances had no fear. That evening we managed, with the help of alcohol, to stay up until ten and then made our way to bed and slept soundly. The next day we kept our appointment with the Celebrant, whose name was Velda and then on Saturday 23rd September, under a palm tree next to the pool in Pam and David's back garden, we married. David and Pam invited some of their relatives to the service, along with their children, and after the ceremony David barbecued a very large fillet of beef. Everybody had a great time, wine and beer flowed freely, the sun beamed down on us and the day was just perfect.

For the next 14 days we travelled around. David was busy at work but did manage to take one day off and drove us to Canberra where all the embassy buildings are built in the styles of the countries they represent, making it a fascinating place to visit. We went into Sydney quite often, and I had to endure the aquarium in Darling Harbour. In the evenings we would sit and watch the Olympics, having agreed to support each other's country when our own didn't have a competitor involved, but as you can imagine there was quite a lot of friendly banter. For the rest of the visit we booked coach excursions. We went to the Blue Mountains, dolphin watching in Java Bay and wine tasting. The wine tasting trip nearly ended our married life before it had begun.

It was our last excursion and was on the day after the Olympic closing ceremony which ran on well into the early hours. We travelled by coach for about three hours to a vineyard and then spent another three hours tasting all the wines on offer. We bought four bottles for Pam and David because this was their favourite tipple, but we came very close to not making it back to Sydney. Our coach driver was a very nice man called Brian and on the way, between his commentaries on interesting places we were passing, he told us he had taken his granddaughter to the closing ceremony and got home at 2am. We had left the coach pick up point at 7am so he had probably only had four hours sleep. On the ride back, after the visit, and both Fran and I were having trouble keeping our eyes open. We were sitting on the front seat of the coach and at one point Frances nudged me and nodded towards Brian who was pouring water over his head and looking very tired. My eyes must have closed for a minute, but when I opened them the coach was travelling at over sixty miles an hour and was weaving from the road onto the hard shoulder. About 50 yards ahead a car had stopped and a young woman and child were standing by its open boot whilst a gentleman was beside the driver's door and we were heading straight for them, furthermore there was a hundred foot drop to the left of the hard shoulder. I glanced at Brian and he was asleep at the wheel so leaping to my feet I shouted...

"Brian, wake up!"

He opened his eyes and swerved violently back onto the road, just managing to keep control. We could not have missed the car and the people by more than a yard. I spent the next thirty minutes talking to him continually and as we alighted from the coach in Sydney he grasped my hand tightly, but neither of us spoke. Fran and I got the train back to Turramurra feeling very thankful to be alive.

On the last day of our holiday David got all the family together and we had to take part in a ceremony to make us Honourable Aussies. This involved being draped in the Australian flag and swearing an oath that we would support any and all Australians in any sport or venture if no Britons were involved. We were then presented with a beautiful wedding album.

At Sydney airport, for the start of our journey home, David took us into a special lounge area and told us they would serve us with any food or drinks we wanted whilst we waited for check in. As the flight was delayed for two hours this was a godsend, but there is a very sad ending to this trip. In Singapore airport, Frances bought a new handbag and after seven years loyal service a very well used tatty bondage bag was discarded on foreign soil never to be seen again; ah!

We arrived home tired but happy, but a shock was waiting for us, or at least, it was a shock to me.

Chapter Twenty Seven: Battle Two

I let go of her hand and as they wheeled her in, I sobbing uncontrollably rushed into the nearest loo...

We opened the front door to my flat at about 8.30am on the 10th October. Our pre-booked taxi had been waiting for us at the airport when we landed from Oz, and as the driver took us to the car I apologised for the delayed flights, but he said it was no problem as they always checked arrival times before they set out. In the communal hallway was a large pile of mail which I picked up on the way to the front door and, then once inside the flat, threw down on the coffee table. We had a quick drink and then tried to get a short nap as it had been more than twenty four hours journeying. When we eventually began to open the mail there were several wedding cards from well-wishers, a few bills and then I picked up a letter from the NHS addressed to Frances Moore, which I thought very strange, and I said...

"Letter here for you from the hospital Fran and it has the surname Moore. How do they already know your new surname?"

"I've sort of been expecting that," she replied. "I went for a breast screening just before we went away and I was talking to the nurses about the wedding and telling them I would have to get used to signing the name Moore instead of Brown, so they must have changed it on my notes. "What does it say?"

We had always been happy opening each other's mail so I tore off the top of the envelope and unfolded the letter inside. The first word I noticed was Oncology.

"What does it say sweetheart?" she asked again.

As I read it my heart sank.

"It says that due to the results of you breast screening an appointment has been made for you at the Oncology Department at QA this Friday at 10am, and what do you mean you've sort of been expecting it?"

"Well I had a feeling all was not well from the looks on the faces of the breast screening nurses, but they didn't say anything to me so I couldn't be sure, and I didn't want us to go away to our wedding with the worry of it hanging over us. Please don't be angry with me."

I wasn't angry; I just wasn't looking forward to Friday and on top of all this I had a booking in Swindon for Sunday service and would have to travel up on Saturday morning.

We still had the rest of the week off work and the following day went to visit my parents. Dad gave us some money as a wedding present and he also wanted Pam and David's address so he could write and thank them for the kindness shown to his son. On the Thursday evening Pat's group, plus a few other friends took us out to our favourite Chinese restaurant and we had a nice evening sharing stories of our Australian adventure, probably boring them all in the process. We kept the other news to ourselves.

On Friday morning the bad news was broken; Frances had breast cancer and would need to have a left mastectomy. The screening had shown extensive crystallization in her left breast and there were no other options available. The breast care nurses said they had known straight away but because of the way Fran had spoken of me they were sure it would not have made any difference to the wedding, so they had decided not to say anything until it was over. Frances seemed so calm, just listened and then asked the consultant about re-constructive surgery.

"I can bring a Naval Surgeon over from Haslar Naval Hospital in Gosport and he can do the reconstruction at the same time as the mastectomy so that you wake up from the operation looking the same as you do now, or you can wait for the reconstruction and have it done at a later date."

Without hesitation she replied: "I'll have it all done at the same time if that's ok."

"I'll arrange for you to have a consultation with Commander Mallion at Haslar within the next few days and I'll get you booked into theatre as soon as possible Mrs Moore, but you may have to wait until Commander Mallion and I are both available at the same time."

When we left the hospital I said…

"You seem so calm Fran, are you ok?"

"To be honest, I knew inside that this was going to happen and so I think I was mentally prepared for it. It's not really the operation that worries me, it's the treatment afterwards that I don't want to think about, so let's just get over this bit first."

On the Saturday I travelled to Swindon and returned home late Sunday evening. When I sat down Fran said…

"A man called Bernard knocked on the door Saturday afternoon and asked if we still wanted to sell the flat."

Great timing!

"What did you tell him?"

"I just said my husband was away for the weekend and if he left me his phone number I would get you to ring him from work Monday morning."

That evening we discussed this development and both agreed that if this was a chance to get out and into a new place then it would be silly to pass it up so, when I rang Bernard on the Monday I had already worked out what I should say.

"We do want to sell the flat but there are a few complications at the present time, so I have to tell you now that the price is £38,000 and if you are not prepared to pay that then there is no point in us going any further."

"I am acting as agent for a builder who has already bought one of the four flats in your building and he needs to buy another so that he can get the freehold. Will it be ok if we both come round and have a look this evening?"

They turned up about 7pm, looked around the flat and then Chris, the builder said…

"Bernard tells me you want £38,000 for the flat, is there any movement in that?"

I replied: None, because if I don't get that price we won't have a deposit for our next home, so it is take it or leave it Chris."

"I think we can do that price, now I gather from Bernard that there may be other complications."

I then explained about Fran's condition and the operation and told him that she would need time to recover before we could go looking for a new place to live.

"Don't worry about that," he said. "We'll go ahead with the purchase as quickly as possible and then you can rent from me at a vastly reduced rate until your wife has recovered and you have found a new home. Bernard can write up a lease contract, but there will be no time limit and no notice required, so you will be able to leave as soon as you have found somewhere. I just want to get the flat so I can go after the freehold."

We couldn't believe it, not only were we going to sell the flat but we were going to be able to rent it until Fran was well again.

Three days later we were in Haslar Naval Hospital with Commander Mallion. We should have been back at work but both employers agreed to let us take another day off, so we could attend the consultation together. Commander Mallion and his head nurse, whose name I cannot remember, were both fantastic people, very down to earth but also very upbeat and encouraging. He examined Fran and then asked her...

"Do you want any adjustment in size and do you want me to perk the other one up whilst I'm at it, or are you happy with how they are at the moment?"

We couldn't help but laugh.

"Just make sure they are both the same size and I don't look lopsided," Fran replied.

A letter arrived a few days later giving a date in the second week of November for the operation. Now we had to inform everybody including Pam and David and e-mail Andrew on board ship. We also had to find out how we stood as far as work was concerned but on that front we needn't have worried. Frances would be given paid sick leave and I was permitted to use Flexi Time as I needed.

Pat came with us to the hospital, mainly to keep me company, as the operation would take about six hours. The QA surgeon, whose name also I can't remember, performed the mastectomy and Commander Mallion worked on the re-construction at the same time. He was going to use the muscle from Fran's back to form the new breast so for the duration of the op she would be laying on her side. We got to the hospital at 8am and were directed to the waiting room while they found Fran a bed. Five hours later the theatre assistant came to talk Frances through the operating procedure, he had to take her into a shower cubical and use the seat in there for them both to sit on. To say I was not happy would be an understatement, but Fran seemed to take it all in her stride. At about 2.30pm a bed became available and Frances was told to get ready for theatre. Within a half hour she was being wheeled to theatre with me beside the trolley holding her hand. This sudden rush may well have made things easier for Fran, but for me it was too much. As we reached the operating theatre I let go of her hand and as they wheeled her in, I sobbing uncontrollably rushed into the nearest loo and locked the door. A few minutes later the porters who had taken her down to theatre were calling out for me to see if I was ok. I managed to pull myself together and made my way back to Pat who was sitting patiently in the waiting room.

"Right," she said, "We'll go into Cosham first, get a bite to eat, go to your parents' house to let them know what's happening and then back to your flat. There is no point in staying here and waiting for six hours, we'll come back this evening."

I have already told you Pat could talk for Britain, but I had never been so grateful for someone taking charge, and talking non-stop for six hours, as I was that day. We went back to the hospital that evening and arrived just as they were bringing Frances back to the ward. As he walked past me Commander Mallion grasped my hand and said...

"It all went very well, if you have any problems with the re-construction don't hesitate to bring her over to me in Haslar."

I went to the bedside to be greeted by one of the breast care nurses who delighted in telling me that they had let her watch the operation and how fascinating it had been. I wasn't really interested because all of my concern was for Fran. I sat with her for an hour, holding her hand, but she wasn't really conscious so the nurse told me I should go home and come back in the morning. I thanked Pat for giving up her day to help me cope, went back to the flat and fell asleep on the sofa. The next morning I made my way onto the hospital ward to be greeted by the sight of Fran sitting up with that beautiful grin spread across her face and at that moment I thought:"Everything is gonna be ok." The surgeon who had performed the mastectomy came to see her and after a quick examination said...

"Everything looks fine and I need to tell you that we did not find any traces of the cancer in the lymph glands or the blood vessels, but I would still recommend a course of chemotherapy to make sure."

Her reply was instant...

"No thank you, if there are no signs of the cancer, I would prefer not to have poison put into my body."

Five days later she was back home with me. While she had been in hospital I had purchased a large sofa bed as I did not want to do any damage by rolling or nudging her in my sleep. The next three months were hectic as we required several trips to Haslar to drain fluid from the re-construction and her back and after a while Commander Mallion decided to take her into the naval hospital as all the trips were beginning to take a toll on our finances. He asked Fran if she would mind them taking a few photographs, so they could be shown to future patients to ease their worries and Fran answered...

"No I don't mind at all. Will that make me the oldest page-three girl in the country?"

We all smiled.

Chapter Twenty Eight: Mother Taken Home

At two o'clock that morning on the 9th June I awoke suddenly to find that Frances was sitting up in bed wide awake...

By February everything had healed nicely, Frances was back at work full time and we were busy looking for a new place to live. We found it quite quickly, not more than half a mile away and another flat, this time two bedroom, although the second one was what is called a box room. The freeholder was an elderly handicapped lady called Mavis and she lived on the ground floor of a house which had been converted into two separate dwellings. We had our own front door and the garden had also been split into two, so we were quite independent, and it was agreed that the cost of any repairs to the outside of the building would be split straight down the middle. Mavis was lovely and she gave us the security number to her front door as we were quite willing to help her at any time. We moved in at the beginning of April and quickly set about making the place our own. We took out a £10,000 loan to have the garden landscaped, so that it was easy to maintain, nice for Fran to sit out under a parasol in the sun and read in the summer months. I employed a chap named Colin, from the Revenue to decorate the two main rooms and he did a good job for us.

Spiritual work in the churches was still bugging me a little and I told Pat that I would not be taking bookings for following years as I needed time for my own progression. She had come to the same conclusion although for her, time for progression was the real reason, whereas for me, I had just become frustrated by those in the churches not going anywhere with their development. Whatever our reasons, we both decided that this was our last year of church services for the foreseeable future, our circles however would continue as normal. Pat also decided to take a four year diploma course on counselling at Portsmouth University to prove to her-self that, as she put it, she wasn't stupid. She went on to pass and, at a later date my sister took and passed the same course.

My mother's health had been gradually declining and one weekend my father woke early to find that she wasn't beside him. He hobbled downstairs to find her collapsed in the front room with a duster in her hand and a can of polish on the floor. He quickly rang Les who called an ambulance and then rushed up to the house to take Dad to the hospital. When I arrived at her bedside the signs did not look good and I honestly didn't think she was going to last the day out, but it is amazing what antibiotics can do and by the next morning she was sitting up looking bright and cheerful. This may have given us all false hope because when she came home she went downhill fast, it wasn't long before she was back in hospital and this time I think we all knew she would not be coming out. Mum was transferred from QA Hospital to St Marys in the beginning of June 2001, and dad would spend his days by her bedside and Les and I would go down after work to be with them. Andy and Frances would be there when they could but we relied on them to look after homes and children. I arrived at the hospital one evening to find Dad and Les sitting beside the bed and Mum awake and seemingly afraid to close her eyes to sleep. She kept on looking up into the corner of the room and calling for her mummy and daddy. I looked at my father and he looked shattered so I said to Les...

"I think you need to take him back to yours and feed him, then take him home so that he can get some sleep."

We spoke to Dad, he agreed and I promised to stay with Mum until she had gone off to sleep. When they had left I took my mother's hand and softly said to her...

"It's ok to close your eyes Mum and if you see a Red Indian just follow him, and he'll take you to Nan and Granddad."

She looked at me and a beautiful smile spread across her face as if she understood, but whether she did I really don't know as she still seemed afraid to close her eyes. I sat with her for about two hours until eventually she couldn't keep her eyes open any longer and drifted off to sleep. I have always regretted leaving the hospital and going home that evening because my instinct told me she would not be waking up, but I suppose I didn't want to believe it. At two o'clock that morning on the 9th June I awoke suddenly to find that Frances was sitting up in bed wide awake, and before we had time to speak the phone rang. It was Andy who told us that the hospital had called and Mum had passed peacefully in her sleep. Les and Andy went to pick up Dad, came for us and we all went down to the hospital together. I went into the room with my father and was a little shocked as nobody had closed her mouth and she reminded me of a horizontal version of the woman in the painting 'The Scream' by Edvard Munch. As I later chose not to see her in The Chapel of Rest this is the last memory I have of her. My father kissed her forehead and told her that she had been a loving and loyal wife and then asked her to wait for him. I managed to hold my tears back until I had left the room to give him his time alone with her.

All the arrangements for the cremation were done as a family, and Dad had her ashes buried in the crematorium gardens under a flower bush because he said that she liked being out in the open air amongst flowers, which was a fact that I had not known about her.

Four or five days after her passing I started to get a high pitched vibration in my ears and began to worry that my mother had not made her transition, so I sat alone with my eyes closed and suddenly she was talking to me. She told me she was not lost but was around to make sure Dad was ok and to let Les and I know she was fine. After this conversation the vibration left me and I knew she was ok. Some months later, I had a very vivid dream in which I died with my mother and was happy to do so.

In November of that year I took my last church service at Cowes on the Isle of Wight, in the same church where I had taken my first service some eight years previous.

Chapter Twenty Nine: Dark Night of the Soul

"You don't understand, I'm not meant to be living this way..."

Now Dad was on his own for long periods as Peter was still working away a lot of the time, I felt it imperative that I tried to see him more than once a week, so quite often after I had finished work I would walk up to the house intending to stay for an hour or so, but every time I got up to leave he would start another story and I would be there for another hour. The trouble was, it would be the same story I had heard the previous visit, even if that visit had been the day before. Loneliness was setting in for him and I knew how that felt, so I didn't mind listening and pretending I hadn't heard it all before.

With Frances having been through so much, and Mum's passing, I decided that we needed a break so I looked at what we had left of the loan and then rang Bernie in Warrington...

"Hi Bern, have you and Eddie had a holiday yet this year?"

"No we were only talking about it the other evening, why?" She replied.

"Do you fancy going somewhere together this September? I know you're good at getting cheap deals and we can go up to a grand, so if you can find us a week somewhere nice that would be good."

"Leave it with me," she said.

I did and she came back with a week in Crete. I told Fran and although the Med wasn't what she would have picked she did understand that we couldn't afford to go gallivanting off to a tropical destination, and the thought of going with her sister made the destination more palatable.

Elsewhere, Jackie and Barry had divorced but remained good friends, and if ever Jackie needed a job done, Barry was always available to do it. Their two children were adults now, had moved on with their lives and I think they just wanted different things, so the parting had been an amicable one. Now her boys were both at school, Les had decided to stop childminding, secured a job in the Revenue and would soon be working on the same section as me. Pat and I decided it was time for the others in the circle to move forward so we told them that one of us would go every other week, but that on the weeks that we weren't there they should take it in turns to prepare and run the circle. When it was Fran's turn she was very nervous but meticulous in her preparation and with each passing turn she grew more confident and would tell me with great enthusiasm all about the evenings when she arrived home. Unfortunately, this was short lived as a few months later she came home feeling very despondent.

"What's wrong?" I asked.

"When you or Pat aren't there nobody seems to be taking it seriously. People are turning up late and then chatting about their children for ages before we start. There is no discipline to it anymore."

During the week Jackie phoned and told me that she was also disillusioned, for the same reasons, and had decided not to sit anymore. After a chat with Pat, I went to the circle the next week and when everybody had arrived, said...

"This doesn't seem to be working. At this moment in your lives you all have other priorities and for both Pat and I the discipline of sitting is the most important part. We have been made aware that this discipline has become almost non-existent when we are not here, so we have decided to pull away and stop sitting. We don't have the right to make your decisions for you, but it seems this circle has become an escape route for some of you, perhaps it's time to focus on your material lives for a while."

There was silence and then Karen spoke up...

"I have to admit that we are always late and there is no excuse for it, as we know what time circle starts and we should get the girls fed and settled much earlier than we do, but we never really make the effort to do so."

Les then chimed in...

"I will say that for me and Andy this has become an evening away from the hustle and bustle of looking after the boys, and I am so tired when I get here that all I want to do is sleep."

After nearly ten years the circle closed, but everybody said, and would still say today, that it had been a huge part of their growth in this lifetime.

Off to Crete for a week with Bernie and Eddie, which was great, but I am glad our hotel room was not like theirs which was infested with large spiders. Bernie couldn't sleep at night because of her fear that they would be crawling all over her. There is very little in this world that truly scares me but since childhood I have been frightened of spiders. I have always said that if you wanted to kill me, without leaving any evidence of foul play, then lock me in a phone box with a spider and I would probably die of fear. Bernie and Eddie had booked themselves another week, so when we left they quickly transferred into our room.

Apart from the odd reading and one more big demonstration for the NSPCC the outlets for spiritual work were now few and far between. The real work had just begun, as now I had to learn to live a material life, in a working environment, and keep to the morals and principles that I had been taught. I was realising that everything that had happened to me was about actually living my truth. I had taken the job at the Revenue because I thought that if this was the way the majority of people wanted to live, and everything in life had a price, then everybody had to pay for it. But after a while, I began to struggle because it seemed that nothing was done fairly. I began to notice flaws in the systems that I had no control over. Whenever I tried to point these flaws out it seemed like very few of those in authority really cared maybe because their orders came from the highest level of government and rocking the boat would jeopardise their family lifestyle. I feel I must point out that in my time at the Revenue my work colleagues were some of the nicest people I have met, and that would include most of the front line managers I worked under.

I would rise at six in the morning so that I could be at my desk by seven which meant that I could leave at three and go home to prepare dinner for when Fran came home. This would sometimes change because I was trying to make up all the flexi hours I had taken when Fran was ill, but there was usually a meal prepared by the time she came through the front door. Because over the years most of my jobs involved me sitting at a desk, and because Fran and I both loved our food (cream cakes were her favourite and any flavour of ice cream mine), my weight had soared and I began to get pains in my back, until one Saturday morning I awoke to find that I couldn't move without searing pain through my spine. Fran called the doctor in who immediately signed me off for four weeks and told me to wait for a physiotherapy appointment, which arrived two weeks later. Luckily Andrew had come home to visit and was able to help me into his car and take me to the appointment. The therapist explained that the bottom two discs had slipped and were trapping the sciatic nerve. It was to be eight weeks before I could return to work, and when I did they had to provide me with a very expensive new chair which would support my back. When I got back, I found that I had been moved onto a new section and that Les and I would be working together.

Andrew had come home to tell us that he and Alison were to divorce. She wanted to leave the ships and have children but he wanted to stay on to further his career, and so they had decided to separate amicably. Fran and I were sad because Alison was a nice girl, but we understood the reasons, and told Andrew to let her know she would still be most welcome to come and see us if she ever came to the UK. Andrew informed us, approximately two years later, that Alison was remarried with children so we were pleased it had worked out for her. He also announced that he had a new girlfriend, Napa a girl from Thailand who was in charge of all the waiters and waitresses on board ship.

That summer Fran and I decided that instead of looking to go abroad we would have six days in London as we enjoyed musical theatre. We booked a cheap hotel and went to a different show each evening: 'Miss Saigon', 'Les Miserable' (Fran's favourite, although she spent the whole time with tears running down her cheeks), 'We Will Rock You' (My favourite) and a couple of others. We had taken day trips to see shows before but this time we crammed a year's worth into the six days and also visited some of the London tourist attractions to fill the daylight hours.

In September 2002 Stuart rang up one Sunday morning to invite us to lunch at a Thai restaurant called the White Rooms which, had opened up on the seafront and, every Sunday would cater a buffet style lunch menu. When we arrived he was sitting with a young lady called Fay who he introduced as his girlfriend. Fay told us they had met on her birthday in 2000 and had been going out together since then. Her birthday was on the 23rd September so they had met on the very day Fran and I married in Australia.

"Why have we not met Fay before?" Fran asked Stu.

"It's only been a couple of years and we didn't know if it was going to last, no point in meeting the parents until we were sure it was going somewhere," he replied.

We just laughed as this was typical laidback Stu.

About a year later Stu and Fay bought a house together in Eastney, which is at the eastern end of the Portsmouth seafront. Fay teaches at the same college as Stu, originally English Language to 15-18 year olds which I found amazing as she is so petite, with beautiful china doll skin, but don't let that fool you because she has a look that can control any classroom. She has since completed a Master's Degree in Archaeology and now teaches that subject.

In the first quarter of 2003 a gentleman called Brian, who used to be on the committee at Shanklin Spiritualist Church, rang me and said...

"Hello Derek, I hope you don't mind but I rang the Temple to get your number. I have broken away from the church and now run a monthly spiritual evening in a hotel in Ryde. I have a meeting this Saturday evening and the lady who was due to take is ill, so I was wondering if you might be available to help me out?"

I thought for a second and then replied...

"I haven't done any platform work for well over a year Brian, if you are really stuck I'll come over but it will be a one off."

On the Saturday evening I found myself on the catamaran from Portsmouth to Ryde, wondering what the hell I was going to do for two hours when I got there. Obviously there would be clairvoyant messages but I had no intention of doing them for two hours, so I would have to talk about something, and for the first time I had no inspiration whatsoever. Brian picked me up from the jetty and drove me the short distance to the hotel.

"Thanks for doing this at such short notice Derek, I really appreciate it. We usually get a good crowd in so I think it should be a good evening."

As I sat in front of a room full of about sixty people and Brian began to introduce me, it felt as if I had never done this before in my life, the butterflies and nerves were as strong as they had ever been.

"I'd like you to welcome our Medium for this evening and I'm sure some of you will recognise him, Mr Derek Moore."

I stood up to a small round of applause, and a few calls of welcome Derek and with no idea what was going to come out of my mouth.

"Good evening, it's nice to be here."

What was going to follow?

"Some of you may remember that I gave up doing this sort of thing over a year ago, and when I did I gave the reason that it was because I needed time for my own progression; that was a lie. I gave up because I had become frustrated with seeing the same faces sitting in the same chairs, waiting for messages and not being really interested in the address. This was wrong of me and went against one of the fundamental teachings of spirit. Who am I to judge when it is the right time for another to go forward, when it is time for them to relinquish that chair or indeed when they are no longer in need of a message, whatever that message may be? I did need to stop for my own progression and part of that progression was to realise I was not as far down the path as I liked to think I was and that this eternal learning ground was not an easy path to tread. Spirit are constantly reminding us that we are spirit here and now, and only when we have learnt to think from our true being do we all think the same. This is why we all have our own unique bodies or machines, to live this lifetime with. This is why each part of those bodies is different, why our personalities are different, why our brains think differently."

There I was, rebuking myself. I was right to come away from the church work for a while but both my motive and purpose for doing so were wrong.

The talk continued, messages followed, and as I travelled back on the catamaran I had a few things to contemplate.

This one evening sparked a difficult time for me. I began to have the same moral dilemmas at work as I had had with my previous employment but, more significantly, deep inside I felt that this was not what I should be doing and as I went through the next 12 months this feeling began to consume my being. Frances was getting stronger physically with each passing month and she began to notice the change in me.

"Where are you going Derek? You seem to have lost your humour, we don't laugh together anymore."

"I don't know babes, I just feel a bit lost at the moment."

One day we were visiting Pat, she began to ask me the same question and I suddenly burst into tears...

"You don't understand, I'm not meant to be living this way, I'm meant to be helping people, not chasing them for money when they have none to give."

The tears were in full flow and Fran grabbed me and held me, but I was feeling no comfort. From the moment this process had started for me, I had found happiness and a real sense of purpose, but at this moment I felt darkness engulf me, and I had no light to show me the way out of it. I would be woken by the alarm at six each morning and sit on the edge of the bed, tears running down my face at the thought of the working day ahead and I had no way out. My light was to come but not in a way I would have ever chosen or wanted.

Chapter Thirty: Our Armageddon

She opened her eyes, lifted her head from the pillow and looked at each of us in turn...

Towards the end of 2003 Frances was playing on the computer and stumbled across a website for Canadian holidays.

"Derek, come and look at this."

I went over and saw an advertisement for flights to Toronto for £49 per person and return flights for £80. We looked up hotels and found that we could book rooms in a three star for £22 per night.

"That can't be right Fran. Is there a telephone number on the website?"

There was, so I called and when I was told that the prices were correct, and included all airport taxes, we decided to book there and then for the following March. This gave us something to look forward to and would help me in some small way to survive the torment of work for the next few months.

Christmas came and went, Les and Andy asked Dad and Peter down on Christmas day and Fran and I went to theirs on Boxing Day. The rest of the break we spent watching box sets of Buffy the Vampire Slayer and the spin-off series Angel. We would sit down at three in the afternoon with plates of buffet style food, and it was very seldom we got to bed before two in the morning because we always wanted to see just one more episode.

Toronto time arrived and did not disappoint. Flights over were comfortable, as was the hotel and Toronto itself is a great city. We took a trip to Niagara Falls and were very lucky as the boat that takes you under the falls (The Maid of the Mist) had just resumed after its winter break. I got to dip my toes in one of the great lakes, something I'd always wanted to do even if it was a bit cold, and we went to the top of the CN tower, a bit scary for me as the lift has a glass door and travels up the outside of the tower. It takes 55 seconds from ground level to the top so I tucked myself at the back of the lift, closed my eyes and counted. When I opened my eyes everyone, including Fran was looking at me grinning, but hey it had worked for me so I didn't care. On the flights home, for another £40 each, I was able to upgrade our seats to Super Economy which made the trip back even more comfortable and we didn't have to pay for drinks.

Memories of the trip managed to placate me for the first few weeks back at work, but then the darkness descended once again and but for the banter and humour of my work colleagues, I think I might actually have gone insane. Fran suggested that as we had enjoyed Toronto so much we should book again for the following March, whilst the prices were on offer and this we did, but March seemed so far away to me that I found it very difficult to get excited. In November Fran came to me and placed some advertising notices in my hand...

"I've made these up for you on the computer, have a look at them and tell me if you want any changes made," she said.

She had produced notices of my intention to run Personal, Spiritual and Psychic development groups in Portsmouth, starting in April 2005.

"What's all this about?" I asked.

"You can't go on like you are Derek, you are living a lie and I hate to see you so unhappy. If you can get three or four groups and run them for two hours each a week, at £10 per person, you can earn as much as you are at the Revenue, and

I know that the rest of the time will be spent preparing the weekly work for them. You are a good teacher who really cares about each individual, and £10 is not an excessive charge for two hours of your time. Have a think about it and then, if you want to do it, we can distribute the notices after the New Year and I can add an actual starting date in April. If you get enough interest, I know of a spiritual centre in Portsmouth where you will be able to hire a room."

"What about work?"

"Do you remember what you said to me when I was at the accountants? We said we would go back to work, not back to misery and unhappiness. If you get enough interest, then just put your notice in and work for yourself."

I thought hard over the next few days and I got the real sense that this work was to be a part of my future, but I also got a very distinct feeling that it was not to be at that time or necessarily based in Portsmouth.

"We'll put the notices out in January and see what happens," I told her.

January came and we placed the notices in the local Spiritualist churches and on the notice boards in shops and supermarkets and waited to see if we got any response. Frances seemed to have caught the usual winter cold, which went onto her chest, but as always she soldiered on. As the cough persisted she took herself off to the doctors in late February, Toronto was looming large and we wanted it to clear up before we went. The telephone had rung a few times with inquiries about the groups and I took names and telephone numbers and told them that when I had enough people I would call them back with more details.

We were due to fly out to Toronto on a Monday so when the last Friday at work came I was feeling so relieved and looking forward to the holiday, but got home to find Fran waiting for me.

"You're home early babes, did they let you leave early for holiday."

"Come and sit down a minute please sweetheart," she said with a serious look on her face. "Derek, I haven't actually lied to you, but there is something I haven't told you."

My heart sank and my head went into a whirl. Had she found someone else? Typical man, but we had always said that if something like that happened we would be upfront and honest before it went any further. She continued...

"When I went to the doctors with this cough he sent me for a precautionary X-ray and I knew by the radiographers face that there was something wrong, so I asked him. He told me that they would send the results through to me, and a copy to my doctor, but I told him I wasn't moving until he had answered my question. He went and got a doctor and they tried to fob me off, but I told them that I didn't want the results sent by post as we opened each other's mail and I didn't want my husband getting a shock, so if I had secondaries then they should tell me there and then. They told me I have tumours in both lungs, but the largest is in my left one. I didn't tell you because I know how much you are looking forward to the holiday and I am unlikely to get an appointment with the consultant until after we get back. Both of the previous times I have known inside that I had cancer, but this time it was as big a shock to me as it is to you; I'm so sorry to put you through all this again. Now we have to decide whether to go to Toronto or stay and wait for the appointment."

There really was no decision to be made, so once I had got my mind in gear I said...

"Don't you ever think you have anything to be sorry for, we've beaten this twice and we'll beat it a third time and then it might just decide to sod off and leave us alone? We'll wait for the appointment because if it arrives whilst we are away we may miss the date and have to wait for another one. We'll keep this holiday time off and not tell anyone until we know what lies ahead; is that ok with you?"

She nodded and said…

"Fish and chips for dinner and then we'll watch that new Buffy box set."

We watched the new box set all weekend without really discussing what lay ahead. Until we had spoken to the consultant we had no idea anyway, so it was a case of trying to take our minds off of it, and Buffy and takeaways seemed to do a fairly good job.

It was definitely the right decision to knock Toronto on the head as the appointment to see the consultant at Haslar arrived on Monday morning, for 3pm on the Friday of that week, so we would have missed it had we gone. I phoned the travel insurance people, explained why we had cancelled the holiday and they said if we sent a letter from Fran's doctor with a claim form, we would get most of our money back. I tried to make the next three days as enjoyable as I could for both of us. We went to bingo and for walks along the seafront and I even relented and went into the aquarium, but to be honest I think we were both walking around in a bit of a daze.

Friday arrived. We took the ferry to Gosport and walked to the hospital which was only a fifteen minute walk from the jetty. After speaking to the receptionist we were asked to take a seat with many others who were also waiting to be seen. We sat in silence and at six o'clock we were still waiting and the room was empty except for us. Fran turned to me and said…

"I think they've left me till last because there is no more they can do for me."

I couldn't answer because I was thinking exactly the same thing.

Cleaners came into the room and started working and then a nurse walked by and noticed us sitting there.

"Are you waiting here for someone?" She asked.

"Our appointment was for 3pm and we've not been seen yet," Fran told her.

She seemed surprised.

"Oh, I thought we had finished for the day. What is your name?"

She then rushed off and came back a few minutes later...

"I am so sorry Mrs Moore; your notes were put in the wrong tray. Please follow me and the doctor will see you now."

We followed her into a side room, where the doctor was waiting, and sat down. He looked up from reading her notes and said...

"I can only apologise Mrs Moore, you must have been sitting out there wondering what the hell was going on."

"If I'm truthful, I thought you were leaving me till last because I'm a no hoper," Fran replied.

"No, no, not at all, there are things we can do to help you, but first we must determine what type of cancer you have. Do you have new spots or marks on your skin that you hadn't noticed before?"

Fran told him she had noticed a purple coloured spot on her scalp and when he looked he said...

"Right, we'll send you up to the day surgery at QA and let them take a biopsy. When the results come through, I'll be able to determine a course of treatment for you and send you an appointment for my clinic in St Marys Hospital over in Portsmouth."

I am not sure how to cover the next six to seven months, simply because I am uncertain how much of the detail of Fran's suffering she would want me to share and also, to be honest, how much of it I want to relive. So here is a précis of that time.

Frances was told that she would have a course of six treatments of chemotherapy at three week intervals. She would lose her hair and there would be other complications and side effects. I was so proud of her, once she knew she was going to lose her hair she went straight to the hairdresser and asked her to shave her head. We then got two free national health wigs and bought bandanas and headscarves. Her body did not react well to the chemo, after every dose the result was the same: for the first two days she was fine, the next seventeen days like a zombie, then picked up for the final two days before the next treatment was due. A portal was put into her arm so that they did not have to try to find veins each time she went, and I would have to wrap this in cling film each morning whilst she showered to keep it clean and dry, but one morning I noticed that her arm was turning blue and so we rushed to the hospital to find that the portal was causing blood clots, so now she would have to inject herself with warfrin every day. I had to get her to the hospital each week to have the portal flushed through, but with all the other complications we were at the hospital at least twice a week anyway, each time sitting staring at the four walls for at least five hours. I couldn't get her to drink enough fluids as to her it all tasted of chemo. We had to pay for all of the medications she took from the hospital and each time we went it meant taxi fares there and back so financially we were getting into a right mess. Nobody told me we could get help with all these costs so I just went on paying by credit card. I knew Fran was worried about the financial situation so I went to the bank and on their advice converted the mortgage to an interest only payment, and combined the credit card costs with what was left of the loan and put it all in my name. I don't really know why I thought this would take some of the worries away for her, but at least not having to pay the full mortgage reduced our monthly outgoings by quite a bit, which helped in the short term. Jan and Nick were also a great help as they would turn up to visit loaded with shopping bags full of groceries and then leave without them.

Both our employers were absolutely brilliant. The Revenue accepted my sick certificates without question and every now and then someone from welfare would ring to see how things were progressing. Fran's employers said they would keep her on full pay for at least six months and then she would go onto half pay. Her best friend at work, Louise was a godsend and made sure that she received everything she was due. Every night I went to bed praying that it could be made easier for her and offering my life in return for her healing. Through all of this suffering she never complained and when the doctor said to her...

"Mrs Moore, I've never heard you ask why me?"

She replied: "Why would I wish this on anybody else, this is mine to deal with."

Sadly, while all of this was going on, we learnt the Jackie was also very ill with stomach cancer and Barry was busy looking after her while her new husband carried on working. Their son lived in a downstairs flat about three doors away from us, and would keep us informed as to how she was doing.

Fran's last course of chemo was at the beginning of December, by which time her hair had started to re-grow which seemed to perk her up. We went to see the consultant on Wednesday the 21st and he said...

"Most of the small tumours are gone but the one in you left lung has not shrunk as much as I would have liked. We have a new drug that I think may help you, called Herceptin, and we will use it in tandem with a different type of chemotherapy. It is put into the body in the same way as chemo so you would come in every three weeks again for six treatments and then on the next day for the chemo. Herceptin does not have the same side effects as chemo. Frances jumped in...

"So it doesn't make your hair fall out?"

"No, Herceptin doesn't, but you will have to sit in the clinic for at least three hours after the first session so that we can make sure there are no adverse reactions to the new drug. I'd like to start this course of treatment tomorrow if that's ok."

Frances looked at him with begging eyes and asked...

"Can I not start after Christmas so I have normality for a few days please?"

He smiled at her and said...

"First treatment on the 28th, now go and have a nice Christmas with your family, but be here by 8.30am next Wednesday."

She went into work on the Friday to catch up with her boss and Louise, and join in with the last day festivities. Christmas day we spent with Stuart and Fay. Fay cooked a delicious dinner with all the trimmings and we played games and quizzes until well into the evening. On Boxing Day we joined Dad and Peter at Les and Andy's house and watched the two boys play with their many presents. It was just like a normal happy Christmas spent with those we loved.

With the reality that both our employers would soon have to cut our wages in half, or stop paying us altogether, we decided that I would return to work until we knew how the new treatment was going to affect Fran. Pat said she would go with her on the 28th as she was going to be at the hospital for at least eight hours and I would take a day's flexi time to go on the 29th when she would have the new chemo. She had no adverse reaction to the Herceptin and so we went the following day for the chemo. As we sat waiting a nurse came over to talk to us...

"We won't be long Frances, we are just waiting for your mixture to come up to us and then we will begin.

"Ok, I am just so relieved I won't be losing the little hair I have this time," said Frances.

"Oh, I am afraid you will, and probably your fingernails and toenails as well," replied the nurse.

"No, no, the doctor said I wouldn't," Fran said with a tremble to her voice.

"I will go and check with the doctor, but I am sure this new chemo has those side effects," came back the reply.

At that moment I saw the fight go out of her as she tried desperately to hold back the tears.

The nurse came back with the bad news. The Herceptin didn't make you lose hair but the chemo certainly did.

After the chemo we went home, but her spirits were low so no matter how much I tried to boost her it was having little or no effect. This chemo did not seem to have the same debilitating effect as the previous mixture so we decided that I should continue going into work. I would rise at six, get ready for work, wrap Fran's arm in cling film so she could shower and get dressed, and then leave. I worked Friday and then we had a long weekend. New Year's Day was on Sunday so I had Monday off in lieu, and then back to work Tuesday. On Friday the 7th of January she had an appointment at the hospital to have the portal flushed through, so I gave her £20 and told her to get a taxi both ways.

"I can get the bus back," she said.

"No you won't, you are to get a taxi and ring me at work when you get home so that I know you are safe."

She rang at about 11am and said she was ok but a little cold so she was going to tuck herself up in bed and try to sleep for a bit. When I got home just after 3pm she was still in bed so I got on and made some dinner. We ate at about 6pm and watched television for a bit and then she took herself back to bed while I stayed up until midnight. When I went to bed she was fast asleep, but when I awoke Saturday morning all was not well.

At this point the actual details of the problems are not really relevant but I will give a brief account of the day.

9am rang hospital who told me that the problems were a normal side effect of the chemotherapy and if I was worried I should phone her surgery's weekend emergency number and ask for a doctor to call.
Phoned doctor who said it was a normal side effect and asked if I really needed him to come. I answered yes and he said he would put Fran on his list of calls.
Finding it difficult to cope I rang Les and she came up to help me, but at midday she had to leave so I phoned Pat who got a taxi straight away.

By 1pm the doctor had not arrived so I rang the emergency number again and was told that the doctors had changed and the one on afternoon duty would be along shortly.
Phoned Stuart and asked him to come up as we might need someone with a car.
Doctor arrived at about 4pm and told Fran she needed to go to the hospital, but he didn't consider it an emergency, had ordered an ambulance and it should be with us within the hour.
Ambulance arrived at 5.15pm and as the two ambulance men took her down the stairs one said to the other...

"We should have been called earlier to this one."

In the ambulance I am asked a lot of questions about her condition and then we set off to QA hospital.
Fran is taken into a cubical on an assessment ward, but by now has lost the ability to communicate.
Nurse comes with an admissions form and asks me the same questions that the ambulance men had asked.
Ward doctor comes and asks me what the portal is for and I tell him. He then asks...

"So she is in palliative care then is she?"

I answer...

"No she is having treatment at St Marys, but nobody has ever said she will not recover."

He quickly examines her and tells nurses to get some anti-biotic drips into her and then takes me outside the cubical and asks...

"So how long has she been in palliative care?"
I give him the same answer trying hard to keep my temper and Stuart is beginning to get angry.

The doctor asks us to go to the waiting area while the nurses try to get the anti-biotic drips set up, but Frances is fighting them and making it difficult.
I take her hand and say...

"If you are in pain babes squeeze my hand."

No squeeze.

"If you are fighting them because you don't want to be here squeeze my hand."

She grasps my hand with both of hers and squeezes tightly.

Doctor ushers us out and says he will call us when they have got her settled, so we join Pat in the waiting area. It is now nearly 8pm.
11.30pm we are still waiting so I phone Bernie in Warrington to explain what's happening and I tell her I'll ring again when I know more.
An hour later I say to Stu that I'm not waiting any longer and we both walk back to the ward where on the wall are Fran's X-rays from St Mary's and beside them X-rays that have just been taken on which both lungs are covered by a large white mass.
I say to Stu...

"I hope that is not the tumours."

A nurse passing says...

"No Mr Moore that is infection".

It is probably a stupid thing to say but at that moment the word infection was a relief to me as I thought, good once the anti-biotic starts to work she'll get better.

Doctor comes over and tells us they are preparing to transfer her onto another ward and as soon as she is settled someone will come and get us and we will be able to see her.
3am a nurse comes and asks us to follow her. She takes us into a waiting room and tells us someone will be in shortly. About 5 minutes later a doctor and a nurse come in and the doctor says...

"Your wife has severe Gastro Enteritis and I am afraid her kidneys are failing fast. If you want me to I can keep her alive for a while by the use of a machine but I am sorry to have to tell you that I don't believe she will see the night through."

I stammered "This is her son I need to discuss it with him."

 Doctor says...
"I'll leave you for ten minutes and then you can tell me what you want me to do and whatever that is I'll then take you to sit with her. She will be able to hear you but don't expect any response."

I looked at Stu and said...

"I think I know what she would want but you have to be in agreement with it."

"I know as well Derek," he replied.

We told the doctor, and he took all of us in to sit with her. At about five minutes to four a nurse showed Bernie and Eddie into the cubical. They had driven from Warrington. I moved to let Bernie sit by her sister and then I said to Frances...

"Look Fran, Bernie and Eddie have come to see you."

She opened her eyes, lifted her head from the pillow and looked at each of us in turn, then lowered her head back onto

233

the pillow and the light left her eyes just as if it had been switched off. I thought: "I've lost her."

So selfish of me to think I've lost her, after all Stuart and Andrew had lost a mother, Bernie had lost a sister and many others had lost a kind, loyal and loving friend, but all I could think at that moment was:" I've lost her."

Chapter Thirty One: Visitant

As I lay there weeping the bed depressed behind me and a body pressed...

We left the hospital and Stuart dropped Pat off on his way home. Bernie and Eddie came back to the flat with me and, while Eddie tried to get some sleep, Bernie and I sat and talked. It was Sunday and nothing could be done apart from trying to contact Andrew. At 10am we drove to Stu and Fay's house. They had already spoken to the Carnival cruise offices in London and they in turn were going to contact Andrew. Later that morning Andrew called us from the ship which was in port preparing for the next cruise. He told us he would be on a flight home that afternoon and would be with us in the early hours of the morning. Stuart said he would come and collect me the following day to take me back up the hospital to collect Frances's things and the paperwork we would need to be able to arrange the funeral. Bernie and Eddie had to go back to Warrington, so I went back to the flat and began the process of letting people know of her passing, including David and Pam in Australia.

The following morning Andrew, Stuart and I decided we would make all the arrangements together as a family, and over the next few days that's what we did. My stepsons were fantastic and looked after me, feeding me and not leaving me on my own for long periods. Andrew did not want to set foot inside the flat, a feeling I could well understand and then there was the fact that his birthday was three days after his mother's passing. How could we send happy birthday cards to a man who had just lost his mother?

Frances was to be cremated on the 18th January and when we went to the funeral directors we had to choose a coffin. Stu said...

"I suppose Mum would have wanted a wicker basket or cardboard coffin?"

"This isn't about what your mum would have wanted, she won't be in it anyway, this is about you and I saying goodbye to her physical presence so you pick whatever you want," I replied.

Stuart and Andrew picked an oak coffin.

Later that day I went to the big insurance company and let them know she had passed as I knew that, although the company itself had been unfair to her, she still had colleagues that liked and respected her there. That afternoon a member of their pension staff phoned and said I would be due a pension from them. This I had not expected.

I was told that the crematorium allowed twenty minutes for each funeral service and after considering who might come, I picked the smaller of the two chapels. I wrote a letter to tell her father what had happened, and the details of the funeral, and sent it to an address I found in Fran's book, but a few days later I received a nicely written letter saying that no one of that name lived at that address.

I didn't want someone who hadn't known Frances to stand up and read words out of a book, with no meaning or relevance to her beliefs, so I decided to write the cremation service myself. After the boys had taken me home I made a coffee and, at about midnight, I sat down at the dining table to start. Trying to say all I wanted to within the twenty minute time scale was proving difficult but eventually, at about 2am, I had finished. All I had to do now was choose the music. Louise and her mother had bought three tickets to see Bon Jovi at Wembley Stadium in June, promising to take Frances if she was well enough, so I knew we would leave the chapel to Living on a Prayer. I had decided that we would enter the chapel to Eva Cassidy's Songbird, one of Fran's favourites, but

I still needed something in the middle for three minutes contemplation time. I was sitting trying to think of an appropriate song when suddenly from the bedroom I heard the sound of music and when I went into the room the small CD player by her side of the bed was playing 'Truly Madly Deeply by Savage Garden'. Not only did I not know we had that CD but how the hell did the machine turn itself on and how did the disc get in there. I suppose Fran could have left the disc in there, but it was not the first song on the album. I sat and listened to the words and they made me cry, but they were not appropriate for the service so I said out loud…

"I'll keep this as our song sweetheart."

In the end I chose Eva Cassidy's version of Over the Rainbow. I took the service to Sue and Richard's house and asked Sue if she would take the service for me, which she kindly agreed to do.

The next evening Louise came to the flat to get the details of the service, and while we were chatting she said…

"I've started the process of Fran's death in service benefit and, as I know you are struggling financially, I have been in touch with the insurers and asked them to process it as soon as possible. It would normally take about three months but I promise you it won't be that long. The company has also decided to pay Fran's salary right up until the end of the month so that will go into your bank account on the usual day. Fran was always worried about how you would survive if this happened, but with the service benefit she knew you would be ok and be able to keep the roof over your head."

Since Fran had passed I had not been able to sleep under the covers of the bed, I would leave the central heating on and just lie on the top. I went to the bedroom that night, sat on the edge of the bed and began to feel anger welling up inside of me…

"Have you chosen to leave me just to ensure I have a roof over my head? You'd better not have Frances, do you hear me?" I shouted through my tears, hitting myself hard at the same time. As I lay there weeping the bed depressed behind me and a body moulded itself into me and arms wrapped around holding me tightly. I looked down to where the feeling of the hands was, but all I could see was a golden glow and I didn't want to move for fear that she may leave me again.

The funeral day arrived and Sue made sure it all went smoothly but I should have booked the larger chapel because it was packed, with many people having to stand. Pat later told me that my father had said he thought it was a beautiful service and then she said that she wanted me to write hers for her when the time came. Fran's ex-husband had asked via Andrew if he could attend and I said I had no problem with that, after all you can't be married to someone for several years and not actually feel something for them. Bernie and Eddie had come down from Warrington and bought Fran's Uncle Tony and Aunty Dot with them, while Les and Andy had kindly offered to hold the after wake or whatever you call it and they did me and the boys proud. Joshua and Dominic acted like grown up hosts and made sure everyone had whatever they wanted. When everybody had left, Andrew took us all out for a meal and then because of work commitments Bernie, Eddie, Tony and Dot all left to drive home, while we went to the pub to get hammered. After putting me in a taxi, at midnight, Andrew said...

"We'll be up to get you for breakfast at 8.30am, so be ready."

I should have known better but by 7.30am I had forced myself, hangover and all into the shower and by 8.15am was waiting for them to arrive. The phone eventually rang about 10.30am and Andrew's weary voice said...

"Sorry mate; none of us are feeling well, but we'll be up later to get you for dinner."

In a way this was fortunate as the 19th was my dad's birthday and sitting on my own I suddenly remembered, so rushed out, bought a card and went to see him for a couple of hours. He never repeated to me what he had said to Pat and I must say that hurt a little.

A few days later Andrew returned to his ship, Stu and Fay returned to their teaching jobs and I was alone for the first time since Fran's passing. Although I was 100% sure she was fine, I knew that all the things we had shared had come to an end, and I feared loneliness was going to set in again.

I went back to work far too early and within three days I was signed off for four weeks with chronic sciatica. I couldn't put my left foot on the floor for more than a few seconds, so couldn't shower, and I had to get a taxi to take me to the doctor's surgery which was no more than 400 yards from the flat. For three days I got no sleep whatsoever as the ache in my leg and foot was so painful and the pain relief tablets did nothing for me. When Fran passed the doctor had given me ten Tamazapan tablets to help me sleep and I had taken none of them, but after three nights without sleep I took one which did help me rest. During those four weeks, Louise called in and gave me a cheque for the Death in Service Benefit and told me there was also a small pension that went with it. The Benefit allowed me to pay off the loan I had arranged with the bank and a large part of the mortgage, and as the insurance company pension also began, I worked out that I could afford to reduce my hours at work to 24 which I had no hesitation in doing.

The year moved on but I'm not sure I did. I have heard it said many times that when you lose someone you love it is like losing an arm, but for me it was as if half my soul had gone, and I knew that it wouldn't be replaced in this lifetime. Les and Pat came and sorted out Fran's belongings for me and the only things I kept were the birthday card and the cheap tea shirt from the cruise which reminds me of the way her face lit up when she was happy.

In July, Jackie lost her battle. Pat and I went to the funeral, which I found very hard being so close to Fran's, and not long after this I was sitting in Pat's front room one Saturday afternoon when, as a throwaway comment, I said…

"Why don't we just sell up and move out in the country somewhere. There's nothing here for either of us."

I wasn't really expecting a reply, but she looked at me and said…

"I wouldn't have the courage to go on my own but if you do it so will I."

From there the snowball gathered pace quickly. Pat placed a pendulum over a map and it pointed to a small town in West Wales. Pat's mother had passed some years earlier and John her stepfather had been left living in her mum's cottage in a little village called Berrow, near Burnham on Sea, and when Pat told him of our intentions he looked very sad as he would often come to Portsmouth to spend time with her. I only knew John as a very quiet man, so when Pat told me I said…

"Why don't you ask him if he wants to join us?"

She did and his response was…

"When do I start packing?"

I know friends and family worried about me at this time, as it all happened so quickly and to be honest they were probably right, but if truth be known, at that point I didn't really care if it worked out for me or not, all I had to lose were material things and money, and I wasn't bothered about either of them. Pat and I sold our places on the same day, completed the sales on the same day and moved most of our possessions into storage in Burnham while we lived with John until his cottage sold in February 2007. My dad's ex-secretary Mary had moved to Wales with her husband Don some years before, where they had renovated an old cottage, but sadly after a long illness Don had passed away. Mary still lived in the cottage with her two dogs Kit and Muffin and she kindly agreed to post the local papers, with all the properties for sale, down to us at John's. We quickly found a house in west Wales that we all liked, moved in on the 23rd May, and a new phase of life began.

Chapter Thirty Two: Living Our Dream

"Our Medium for this Saturday has let us down so I wondered if you would be kind enough...

The house we bought is a newly built four bedroom dormer bungalow on the outskirts of a small village three miles west of the university town of Lampeter. Behind the house is a thirty foot high bank and at the front a large wide drive at the side of which is a twenty foot drop into a quarter acre meadow leading down to a river. Although there is a road passing us it is only busy at the beginning of the working day and for a short time each evening when people are travelling home. The front of the house faces out over the meadow and river, and the bird table is always busy feeding woodpeckers, nuthatches, goldfinches and many other species of birds. In the middle of the meadow is a tall ash tree where buzzards often come to sit while red kites circle over the house, gliding on the currents of air. Some fifty yards up the road is a quiet country inn which was run by a kind husband and wife team who have now retired, but for the first few weeks this was our eating establishment whilst we settled in, unpacked, waited for floors to be carpeted and had the great fun of trying to get a telephone line connected. When we first moved in we had terrible problems with the plumbing, but Mary put us on to a great plumber called Gary who soon got everything sorted and, despite a few disputes with the builder, this was and still is the house and countryside that Frances and I had often talked and dreamed of.

As I unpacked, I came across the advertising notices that Fran had printed for me, and I decided that I would try to put our plan into action in this new environment. After making the necessary adjustments to the notices, I found a spiritualist church in a little harbour town called Aberaeron which is about 13 miles from the house, and finding out that they held their service on a Saturday afternoon I took myself, with my notices, there by bus. After the service I stayed for a coffee and spoke to Sandy, the lady who ran the church, about putting up my notices.

"So you are a Medium then?" she asked.

"Yes" I replied.

"I'll introduce you to our Medium secretary Bernice then, and she can book you for next year."

I didn't really want to go back on the platform, but decided that, as it wasn't till the following year and there were very few Spiritualist Churches in west Wales it was only liable to be the odd one or two services a year, and I could always stop if they became too much. I put my notices up and made my way home. On Monday morning the three of us drove into town and went to our favourite cafe for breakfast. After eating I left Pat and John and wandered around putting notices in different shops and in the local council offices and when I had done this I sent up a thought to spirit; if this is what I am meant to be doing, find me the people. I also began looking for a room to hire as John did not share the same beliefs as Pat and I, so it would be unfair of me to use the house and ask him not to watch television and keep quiet for two hours each week.

Wednesday evening the phone rings and a quiet voice asks...

"Can I speak to Derek please?"

"Speaking," I replied.

"Oh hello Derek this is Bernice from Aberaeron Spiritualist Church."
"How can I help you?" I asked.

Silly boy.

"Our medium for this Saturday can't come, so I wondered if you would be kind enough to fill in for her."

Before I knew it, I had agreed, and so on Saturday afternoon I found myself taking the service which went very well despite feeling as nervous as I had the first time, all those years ago.

Coincidently, that is if you believe in coincidence, a man named Graham who had taken the same diploma course as Pat moved to Lampeter just one week after us with his partner Stuart whose sister Kate lived in Lampeter with her young daughter Rosie. They had bought a large seven bedroom house just behind the main High Street and one Sunday we asked them over for lunch. I cooked a beef roast and they bought the wine. As we were talking I mentioned that I had been looking for a room to hire without success and Graham said...

"You can rent our front room if you want to. Stuart works away during the week and I can always go to Kate's in the evening, so you will have full use of the ground floor."

Perfect; we agreed on a price of £20 for the evening and I waited to see if I got any interest from the leaflets. Five weeks passed and I had only had two bites, one from a lady called Carol who would have to travel 36 miles each way to come, but said she was willing to do so, and one from a young woman called Jess who had seen me at Aberaeron Church. I took telephone numbers and said I would call with details if and when I had the required number of people.

As we all began to settle into our new environment I started to make my bedroom into my living quarters. Pat and John were linked by family and liked to watch the same things on television, whereas I just flicked around the stations seeing if there was any sport to watch, so it made sense to me to let them have the front room. I was quite happy in my bedroom which was large enough for a table with comfy chair and I also had my own en suite shower room; it was a bit like having my own flat again. I took on the task of cooking and helping Pat with the cleaning, while John took charge of the meadow which he would mow with a hand mower. This would usually take him all afternoon but when we offered to get him a sit on mower he said he didn't want it and was quite happy to do it the old fashioned way. Pat and I registered with the doctors' surgery and the dentist but John wouldn't transfer from his doctors or dentist in Weston Super Mare and said he would drive back every three months, as he had prostate cancer which was kept under control by quarterly injections. Flora and Finlay were settling in well and Fin couldn't believe his luck as he set about claiming his territory and providing us with presents of mice each morning.

On Saturday mornings I would take the bus to Aberystwyth and walk along the seafront on my own as it got me out into the fresh air and gave me my own space to think. I had put the notices out five weeks before and had still only had the two responses, and as I walked along the promenade I began to wonder if I had done the right thing. John wasn't the quiet man I had taken him for, and some of his radical views were a cause for concern to me and I knew that if Fran was still with me we would most definitely have not moved here with him, but at the end of the day my understanding told me that everyone has a right to an opinion. When I arrived back home Pat said...

"A lady called Pam rang and said she had six people who would be interested in your group, so I've taken her number and said you would ring her this afternoon."

I rang Pam and she told me that she helped run a spiritual centre in a place called Llandysul, about 10 miles south of Lampeter. I gave her a date and time for an informal evening where over coffee and a biscuit I would explain what I was offering and then they could make their minds up as to whether it was what they wanted or not. I then telephone Jess and Carol with the same info and arranged with Graham for the use of the room. At the informal meeting I met everyone, except Jess who was unavailable that evening, but after a chat on the phone she said she wanted to be included in the circle. The circle started on a cold winter's night in November 2007 and Fran's dream for me had become a reality.

Untold riches

Except for the rings that bound us
Gold, silver, or diamonds I never had
Nor wanted
The treasure of this life was finding you
Three times big C came calling and twice we were victorious
Third time it won the battle
As I watched the light in your eyes go out
I knew that although the machine was broken,
Your spirit was free, and all that you were
You still are and always will be.
I used to think you had been brought to me to learn
So battered and bruised.
Egotistical idiot
Now you are gone I realise how much you taught me
I hope it is in equal measure
I try to live the life we spoke of
To some small success I pray
I have died with you in dreams and hugged you tight
But when you return in conscious times and hold me close
I understand how rich I am.

Chapter Thirty Three: The Hotel Opens

"Do you mind if I stay here with you for a while please...

At the end of 2006 Peter had taken early retirement and was at home looking after Dad who was now well into his eighties. He had been diagnosed with Glaucoma and had then had shingles which spread from his head into his right eye. He also had prostate cancer, although this was under control through medication, but he had become incontinent so had a catheter bag attached to one of his legs. His main way of getting around was by mobility scooter and he had two of these, one for getting to and from shops and his church, and one that Peter could fold up and put in the boot of the car so they could have days out if they wanted to. Peter had also had a stair lift fitted to make life easier for both of them.

In September 2007 Peter rang me and asked if he and Dad could come and stay for a week and after clearing it with Pat and John we set a date in October. I gave up my room so that Dad had his own shower and loo close, while Peter booked a room at the pub. I moved into the spare bedroom for the week. Just before they came I hatched in my mind a cunning plan to give Dad and Pat time together so he could get to understand her better. During the daytime we took dad out to various places of interest and he would bomb around the shopping centres in Carmarthen and Aberystwyth on his scooter nearly knocking people off the pavement as they tried to avoid him. On the Tuesday evening, knowing that Dad didn't drink, I said to Pete and John...

"Do you two fancy a pint up the pub?"

John would never turn down a pint and Pete was up for it so off we went leaving Dad alone with Pat for a couple of hours. When we got back everything seemed congenial so I suggested that on the Thursday evening we all went up the pub for a meal after which Pete, John and I stayed for a pint, while Pat and Dad went back to the house. My plan seemed to be working, but I might have gone a bit too far. Pete and dad were due to leave on the Sunday morning so the three of us went back to the pub for a family dinner on the Saturday evening. After we had eaten I said to Pete…

"If you'd like to walk Dad back to the house and then bring John back here, I'll get the drinks in."

Dad looked across the table at me and, with a pleading look in his eyes, asked…

"Do you mind if I stay here with you for a while please?"

"Of course you can," I replied and then asked, "Are you ok?"

"Yes I'm fine and I've had a really nice week. I can see why you have moved here and I must say that I could easily spend the last days of my life in these peaceful surroundings. I can also now see where you're coming from. In Pat I see a really nice, kind and thoughtful lady, but my god can she talk and unfortunately she has the biggest inferiority complex I have ever come across."

I looked at him and smiled.

After they had gone home Pat said to me…

"I really like your Dad; we had some good conversations while you were up the pub. He told me he had come up to see the house and to make sure his son was happy and he was going home with his mind at rest."

The group was becoming established and everybody seemed committed, except Pam who, after the first week decided it wasn't for her and had left. My sitters were a lady called Mary and her daughter Marie, Clair, the wife of our plumber Gary, Jane, Carol, Jess, Beryl and a couple Sharon and Eric. Within a few weeks they had all bonded and it had become clear to me that most of them were there to gain the self-worth and confidence they needed to change their lives. This was not the case for Sharon and Eric as Sharon was already a well-grounded Medium, all she needed was to realise it herself. I had suggested to the two of them, along with Beryl, that they might like to sit to develop trance and they jumped at the chance. We began to sit once a fortnight at Sharon and Eric's house and Pat also joined us. One evening after circle, Sharon said to me...

"I hope you don't mind Derek, but Eric and I have decided to leave the circle at Graham's house. We feel that after sitting in England for many years we have covered much of what you are doing at the moment. I hope you are not offended because we still want to continue with the trance circle."

"I'm not offended at all, I just want to know what has taken you so long; you could be running groups like this," I replied.

The rest of the group were to sit with me for over four years and three of them were to go on to find that confidence and change their lives dramatically. I can't give more details without betraying the confidences of the circle and I am not prepared to do that. I started a second group, at the spiritual centre in Llandysul, and a couple of the girls there also made big changes to their lives. What I will say is that all of these people were willing to look deeply at themselves, and everything that happened for them was down to their willingness to be patient and connect with the spirit within, which then changed the way they thought. All I did was to give them a safe environment to make those changes.

Pete and Dad coming opened the floodgates as far as visitors were concerned and the house became like a hotel. Peter came back twice the following year, but would always stay at the pub because he wanted his own bathroom and a bit of space. Les and Andy came for the first of their many visits, as did Barry and friends of Pat who seemed to come in threes. We seemed to be constantly stripping beds and washing sheets and duvets. I used to feel guilty because John had nobody to visit him but still had to put up with all our visitors. I have to be honest and say that I thought they would all come once out of curiosity, and then not bother anymore. How wrong I was.

Pat and I were discussing the tall ash tree which stood in the middle of the meadow and we decided that we needed to get in touch with a tree surgeon as when the ground had been excavated some of the tree's roots had been cut through and some of its branches looked to be dying. Mary gave me the number of a friend of hers and I rang and left a message on the answer phone asking him to ring me. On the Wednesday of that week I received three calls during the day from an Indian man claiming to be from the computer company and telling me there was something wrong with my computer. The first two times I politely told him I wasn't interested in what he had to say and put the phone down. On the third occasion I told him again politely that he was a scammer and I didn't want any more calls from him. That evening I went off to the group at Graham's and returned home about 9.30pm, and after saying hello went straight up to my room. A few minutes later Pat knocked on my door, came in and perched on the edge of the bed and speaking very quietly said...

"Derek I have to tell you that we've had two phone calls this evening from that Indian chap. I took the first one and was very blunt with him, but the second time John snatched the phone from me and shouted very racist comments at him until he put the phone down."

"Oh, I don't believe there is ever a reason for those sorts of comments no matter how annoyed you may be, but there is nothing you or I can do, that is John's to deal with," I replied.

The following morning as I was drinking my coffee the phone rang and when I picked it up it was Mary.

"Hello Derek, is John in the same room as you?"

"Yes" I replied.

"Well I won't dwell on this but I just have to let you know that my friend called twice last evening about your ash tree and on the second occasion he was subjected to the most vile abuse, so needless to say he won't be coming to look at the tree. I'll just leave it with you."

My stomach began churning and when I walked into the lounge to replace the phone Pat saw my face...

"What's up?"

I told her and her face dropped.

"We must have mistaken his accent. I was blunt but I wasn't rude," she said.

"I'll have to speak to John over breakfast," I replied.

John and I went into the cafe for breakfast and when we had finished eating I told him what Mary had said. He looked up at me and all he said was...

"Oh well, guilty as charged."

I went home and after getting the gentleman's address from Mary I wrote a letter saying that it was not my place to apologise for other people, but I was sorry because nobody should be subjected to that kind of abuse and I hoped my housemates would forward their own apologies. To her credit Pat found the courage to phone him and apologise but she wasn't really sure that it had been accepted. John just said he didn't apologise to anyone and tried to pretend it was macho instead of the actions of coward. Later that week John drove back to Weston Super Mare to see his doctor and have his three monthly injections and while he was gone Pat said to me...

"I can't understand it Derek, I've known John for over forty years and although I knew he held racist views, I have never known him to be so rude to people. I didn't tell you but when Graham came round earlier in the week, John was very rude to him as well."

The reason was shortly to be revealed.

Unfortunately, we lost Flora as her back legs failed and after a few days to see if she could rally Pat asked John and me to take her to the vet to be put to rest. She had been Pat's companion for over 16 years, or should I say Pat had been her companion, either way Pat was devastated. Two months later Graham and I bought her a small tortoise-shell kitten, which she named Dora because apparently Dora means gift. Finn then set about making sure Dora knew that he was now boss of the household and she would have to take her place below him. It was quite funny to watch the process.

Chapter Thirty Four: A Letter to my Father

"I asked you to come down so I can say goodbye because I'm dying...

As we went into the second year in our new house John's moods were very variable and this took me back to those childhood weeks of treading on egg shells due to Dad's mood swings. I did however have some understanding of Dad's dark hours, whereas I had no idea what was causing John's. The only time this changed was when Pat's friend Martin came to visit. Pat and John had known Martin since the early years before Pat's marriage, and his relationship with John was like father and son. John seemed to come alive when Martin was around and it was nice to see him with that bond. The three of us were sitting at the breakfast table one Wednesday morning when I thought I would try to lighten the atmosphere by making a suggestion...

"Who fancies a day out in Cardigan and then a trip along the coast back to Aberaeron for lunch?"

Pat said she and Graham were off to Carmarthen so she couldn't go, but John seemed quite enthusiastic so the two of us set off in the car. As we drove I began to notice that John didn't appear to be using the gears properly but we made it to Cardigan, which was about a 35 mile journey and after parking the car, walked around the shopping centre and found a nice cafe for coffee. The conversation between us was very sparse as John only spoke or answered in one or two words and it was quite difficult trying to keep a dialogue going. After coffee we began the journey back to Aberaeron but we had not been going long when the engine started to overheat, so John pulled into a supermarket car park to let it cool. Fifteen minutes or so later we continued our journey, had a fish and chip lunch and then went home. On Friday Pat was going out again so I said to John...

"Come on mate I'll buy you lunch."

"Sounds like a good idea," came back the reply.

"If we just go up to the pub you can have a drink and won't have to drive anywhere," I said.

So we set off on the short walk up the hill to the pub. Now John was 72 years of age but he was as strong as an ox and he walked a lot faster than my fat body would allow me to. As I reached the door to the pub I suddenly realised that John was lagging behind and when I turned I noticed he was dragging his left leg up the hill.

"You ok mate?"

"Yeah fine, get the beers in."

I got the drinks and we ordered lunch but when I had finished John was only halfway through his, which was again unusual. When Pat came home I said to her...

"I don't think John's well."

"I've been thinking that for a while but you know what he's like, every time I ask him if he's ok, he just says he's fine," she replied.

As the weeks passed he became more and more estranged and when he came downstairs in the mornings would sit in his chair in the living room and not move until I called him for dinner. He seemed to forget that he smoked or drove so Pat hid the cigarettes and his car keys. One morning she went into the living room and sat down next to him.

"John, I'm worried, I don't think your well and I'm going to get someone to come and see you."

He didn't speak but nodded so Pat phoned the surgery and asked for a doctor to call in as soon as possible. When he arrived, he examined John and then said he was going to phone an ambulance, to take him to Carmarthen hospital to be checked over, because although he could raise his arms and speak, he thought he may have had a small stroke. He was at the hospital all day and at 9pm the phone rang and it was John...

"They can't find anything wrong with me can you come and pick me up now?"

"Can you put the nurse on the line John?" Pat asked.

When the nurse answered Pat explained that neither of us drove so we couldn't pick him up and the nurse replied...

"I'll get one of our volunteer cars to bring him home. The tests we've done are inconclusive, so we have made him an appointment for Monday at the stroke clinic. We'll arrange transport for him, which should be with you about 8.30am."

We didn't reach Monday as when Pat got up on the Sunday and passed John's bedroom, she saw him sitting on the floor unable to get up. We managed to get him into bed and I phoned for an ambulance which came promptly and took him back to Carmarthen hospital. The ambulance men told us to wait for a call as they thought he would be in overnight. Later that day a nurse rang and told us we should go to the hospital in the morning to speak with a doctor. When we arrived, the doctor said...

"I'm afraid John has a large tumour in one of his lungs and we have found five lesions on his brain and that is only the ones we can see. I am sorry to tell you there is nothing we can do for him except make him as comfortable as possible."

Pat spent nearly every day at the hospital for the next six weeks until John passed away in November 2008. He had already arranged his funeral, as he wanted to be buried with Pat's mum, back in the village of Berrow. Graham came to stay and look after the cats while Pat and I went to the funeral. John had been estranged from his two brothers from the age of 17, but one of them, Willy and his wife Rose, did come from London for the funeral, but there were only seven people there which I found a sad experience. Willy told us that his older brother was dealing with his own fight against cancer and he knew John was in touch with him via the odd phone call, but Willy had not seen or spoken to him for over 50 years.

After John's passing I moved the group away from Graham's and into home and I also put out notices to see if I could start a second one. Before long I had nine people interested and then I had an idea. Since we had moved, except for the trance circle Pat had been idle as far as the spiritual work was concerned, so I offered her the chance to run the second group and she was pleased to do so. This got her moving and soon she was taking the odd service in the churches as well.

The New Year came and bought more sad news when Tatiana rang from Germany to tell me her father, my friend Werner, had passed through stomach cancer. As the year rolled on both groups settled down and it was nice that twice a week this big house was full of the sounds of chatter and laughter. We didn't see Barry, as he had decided to go and live in Spain for a while, but Les and Andy came to stay in June, and then Peter came up on his own as Dad was not well enough to travel five hours in a car. When he was here he said to me…

"Dad has asked me to say he would like you to come to Portsmouth, because he wants to speak with you."

I packed a bag and went to Portsmouth to see him, thinking I could also catch up with Stu and Fay and cousin Chrissie while

I was there. I booked into the hotel and went to Les and Andy's for dinner and the following morning went to see Dad. We sat and chatted for a while and then he turned his head to me and said…

"I asked you to come down so I can say goodbye because I'm dying. I haven't done much for you; your mother brought you all up really."

I didn't know what to say to him, it was true he was dying, but the second statement concerned me a little, however before I had time to think he had changed the subject and was telling me one of his stories. When I got up to leave that day I would have loved to have given him a hug, but I was unsure as to how he would react and he was in a very frail state, so I just placed my hand on his shoulder and squeezed a little. When I got home to Wales I sat down to write him a letter and I'll share that with you now.

Hi Dad.

It was really good to see you and I hope this finds you as well as can be expected and in good spirits.

It's a bit of a strange feeling when your dad asks you to come so he can say goodbye because he's dying. You can't really say don't be silly, because as much as you wish it wasn't so, you know it is and you don't want to say goodbye to someone that has been a part of your life forever. Circumstances change in life, but your parents stay constant, and even if you don't see them for long periods of time there's this inner knowing that they are always there when you need them. At least for me that's always been the case.

I suppose it might be true to say that at certain times in our lives we reflect back to assess our journey, and look at who we really are, and how we have handled and dealt with all the experiences that this life has presented to us. The last few times I've visited and we have talked, you have seemed to be reflecting on yourself as a man and as a parent in a very negative way, so your 55 year old son is just going to put you straight on a few things.

From the moment we are born into this world every situation and experience is new to us. We watch and learn from our parents because they are our guardians, but what we don't realise at that point is that us just being there is a new experience for them and they are learning as well. The thing with this learning lark is that it ain't as easy as we like to think it is, and we all struggle at times trying to be perfect, when perhaps if we were that perfect we might have no need to be here in the first place. But it is a strange thing this perfection, because it isn't always what we perceive it to be. So let's get a few things straight or at least this is how I remember it. I have a father who worked his butt of to keep me, my mother, my brothers and my sister safe, well fed and well clothed. I have a father who through his example tried to teach me honesty, integrity and to respect others, and if now I have half as much of those qualities as you have, then I'll consider myself to be an 'alright person'.

I watched and listened over the years I worked at Marconi, and was proud of the respect and high regard in which my father was held by everyone from secretaries to managing directors. I have also admired his generosity to those who had less than him and his willingness to help others. It would be true to say that I married a woman who had those same qualities, and it would also be true to say that it doesn't take much looking to see them in both Lesley and Peter. I can't talk for David, as since our teenage years I have very rarely seen him, which is as much my failing as his. I am also drawn to those qualities in the people I call my true friends. So as far as I'm concerned, my mum was the perfect mum for me and my dad was, and still is the perfect dad for me. Because of you and Mum I am who I am today, and I quite like me, and I know through the people I now try to help that people who can say that truthfully are few. Over the past 20 years I have had people come and talk to me who have made me feel quite humble, and made me appreciate the upbringing and childhood I had.

Because of the experiences I have had over the past 20 years I know for sure that we exist outside of this physical being, so therefore I know for sure that goodbye is not forever. There is a lot more I could say but I don't think you want pages on my philosophy of life, because in all honesty I don't think we differ as much as you may think. So just be aware that as a man and a spirit, and most of all as my dad, I admire, respect and love you very much and as you reflect on this life do so in a positive way, remembering not just the faults that all humans have, but also the many qualities and good things you've accomplished.

God Bless

Love Derek. x

Dad past away in a local hospice in October 2009, he was 89 years old. The chapel at the crematorium was full as family and friends came to say goodbye to a decent honest man who I loved.

The year ended with my circle coming to a natural end. Mary and Marie had found new partners and were to move away from Wales. Clair was recovering from a major operation and Jess was in the process of making big changes to her life. All of them told me that without the circle these changes probably wouldn't have happened.

Chapter Thirty Five: Déjà vu

She hadn't fallen; just lain herself down and placed her head on the step...

I think that if, after Fran had gone, I had known what was going to happen in the following six years I might well have said to spirit: Get me out of here now," because, as we entered 2010, I began to notice changes in Pat and around March of that year I was getting worried. She seemed to have lost a lot of weight in a short amount of time and become very uninterested in food. She took herself off to the doctors and then went to Carmarthen hospital for test after test, but they couldn't find anything wrong, until a blood test in May revealed she had Non-Hodgkin's Lymphoma and the cycle started again with Chemo every three weeks. This could have been an especially awkward time for me because Pat and I were not a couple and, if she had the same problems as Frances, she obviously wouldn't want me to be helping with any personal problems. Thankfully, two ladies from the village, Denise and Tess, told me that if I needed help at any time of the day or night I could call on them. Obviously Pats group and the trance circle had to stop until she was well.

Pat's reaction to her chemo was almost immediate, her appetite picked up and she began to feel physically better, although it did make her tired. As with Frances, I had to make sure she took her medicines at the right time and, for the first two weeks after each chemo session, I restricted visitors who had any semblance of an illness as her immune system would be very low. Pat, like Fran, found a local hairdresser to shave her head and provide wigs, bandanas and headscarves. A lady from her group called Annie, and her husband Brydon, were a godsend as they would give up their time to take her to and from hospital on the days of her chemo and I would feed them all when they got home. Annie and Brydon visited most Sundays for a chat over tea and biscuits and Graham would come once a fortnight to help me with the cleaning.

As the end of the year approached the doctors decided to send Pat to Cardiff hospital to spend a couple of weeks having stem cell treatment which, if I understood correctly, meant they would harvest cells from her body, clean them and then replace them. Jan phoned to tell me that Nick was also in hospital, in Portsmouth, and the signs were not good. This was the year it snowed well before Christmas and after Pat's treatment the return transport was unable to bring her home. It looked as if she would be spending Christmas in hospital, but luckily the weather relented long enough for them to get her home just in time.

In March 2011, she went back into Cardiff hospital for more treatment and whilst she was there, Peter phoned me with the shock news that my brother David had died, just before his 60th birthday. He had fallen asleep on the sofa, which was something he did quite often, so Lynn left him there and went to bed. When she went down in the morning he had passed from a massive heart attack.

David's funeral was the day before Pat was due out of hospital so I couldn't go. Lynn understood and said I had to look after the living, but it wasn't easy for me, and on the day I said my own prayers for him.

Mary took me down to pick-up Pat, but in mid-April the three of us set off once again for Cardiff as Pat received a letter asking her to keep an appointment with the consultant. I went in with her and the consultant explained they would just like to do a few tests which would take about three hours. Pat went off with the nurses and Mary and I set off to explore Cardiff for a couple of hours, but to be truthful, we just drove around and stopped for a sandwich and coffee before returning to the hospital. I found Pat, who was waiting to see the doctor for the results of the tests. When we went in the doctor was smiling and said...

"We can only see few faint spots of the cancer left and we would like you to come back in a month's time for one more session, just to make sure we clear it all."

Pat looked stunned so I butted in with…

"So are you telling us that she is in remission?"

"Yes she is. We'll send you an appointment for your last treatment."

We went down to the large reception area to tell Mary and then took the long drive home with joy in our hearts, stopping for fish and chips to celebrate the good news. A couple of weeks later, Pat got a date in late May for her last session. At home, it seemed as if a bit of normality had returned as we were going into town for breakfast and Pat was spending her money on new plants for the garden. It was cup final day, May 14th, and I had my afternoon planned so we went in for breakfast, looked around the shops and then came home in good time. At three o'clock I said…

"I'm going up to watch the football. I'll come down and make a cuppa at half time."

"Ok, I'm going out to plant the honeysuckle I bought this morning," She replied.

The first half of the football was hard going. I went downstairs to the kitchen to make the drinks and looked for Pat in the front room. She wasn't there, so I went into the kitchen, filled the kettle and went to the back door to see if she was still in the garden. The backdoor was open and at first I didn't see her, but then I saw her head on the doorstep. She hadn't fallen, just lain down and placed her head on the step. One look told me this was serious so I rushed for the phone and dialled 999. As I stood beside Pat the lady on the other end of the phone started asking questions, which I tried to answer, then the ambulance arrived and the two men took over. I phoned Mary to ask for her help once again and, after making sure the cats were ok and the house was secure, we followed them to Carmarthen hospital. On arrival we were shown to a family room and waited until the door opened and a doctor and nurse came in together. I turned to Mary and said...

"I've been here before, I know what this means."

The doctor explained...

"We took Mrs Pitcher straight for a scan and I have to tell you that she has suffered a massive brain haemorrhage, I'm sorry to say that there's no coming back from it."

The nurse then took us to the ward room and left us with her. After half an hour or so I said to Mary...

"I can't leave her but you must go home to your dogs, I'll phone Graham to tell him and ask him to go to the house and sort the cats out for the night."

"Are you sure?" She asked.

"Yes, I could be here all night so you go on home."

"Ok, but I'll sleep with the phone next to me and if you need me to come and pick you up just call."

Mary went off home and after I had phoned Graham, I sat with her until she passed at about 2.30am on Sunday. Mary came and took me home but I couldn't go to bed, I made coffee and sat in the silence. The morning came and I didn't know where to start, so I got her phone book and after letting her relatives in Weston-Super-Mare know, I worked my way through the book.

Andy came up for a week, to help me sort out her affairs, arrange the cremation service, which I wrote as I had promised her I would. I also asked Sue in Portsmouth to organise a memorial service at the Temple for her about a month after the funeral. I asked Sandy, the president of Aberaeron church, to take the service and even though we were miles away from Portsmouth the crematorium chapel was full. The crematorium at Aberystwyth is beautiful and has a full wall window that looks out over a valley. As the service started a red kite flew up from the valley and passed across the window; a fitting tribute to her. Pat's relatives, Grace and Michael, said I had done a good job and after the usual do at the pub, they made their way back to Somerset, but I had a houseful of people who had come from Portsmouth, including one girl who pitched her tent in the meadow. Barry had come over from Spain and he asked me…

"What are you going to do now mate?"

"I have not got the faintest idea Barry, I know I can't afford to stay here in this house on my own, but I don't want to go back to Portsmouth, I love it here and I like the people I've met. I can survive for about a year, but if I am going to put the house on the market I'll have to do it soon as houses take so long to sell here."

A few weeks passed and Grace and Michael came to collect the family heirlooms. Sharon and a couple of Pat's group helped sort out the rest of her belongings. I went to Portsmouth for the memorial service, which saw many people wanting to say good things about her. While there I saw Les and Andy and they expressed an interest in coming to Wales to live when Dominic had gone off to Drama school, in three years' time, as they loved it when they came to visit. I told them that providing I could survive the three years, I would sell them half the house and that would enable me to give Andrew and Stuart a small part of their inheritance early, and give me a safety net until I reached pension age. On returning to the large, empty house, I received even more bad news, when Jan phoned to tell me Nick had passed. There I was, alone again, not knowing how I could possible keep the house for three years, but my salvation was not long in coming.

Chapter Thirty Six: Family Finale

"Is it ok if I come up for a fortnight in February to look at a few houses...

Home from Pat's memorial, I was rattling around in the house, trying to work out ways and means of surviving financially for the three years until Les and Andy could join me. Over the previous few weeks they confirmed that they would like to come, but it would be impossible before Dom had left for Drama School. One sunny afternoon in July my mobile phone rang and when I picked it up a friendly voice said...

"Hello mate, just ringing to let you know I'll be with you at the end of August. I've put notice in to leave the apartment here in Estapona and I'm coming to live in Wales for a while, so make sure you get my room ready."

Good mate Barry arrived and a lot of the pressure was off. I explained to him about Les and Andy coming and told him that when it happened he didn't have to leave as he would have a home here for as long as he wanted. The first Saturday after his arrival we both went to Jess's wedding in Aberystwyth, it was good to see her so happy. Barry settled in quickly and his whistling and the sounds of him practicing playing his keyboard became part of everyday life in the house. I used to upset him by telling all our visitors that he had been playing with his organ all morning. The girls in the cafe in Lampeter already knew him from his regular holiday visits and we wasted no time in joining the bowls club, although the weather restricted our actual playing time. We also spent hours playing golf on the X box we treated ourselves to for the first Christmas, and Barry's daughter Kate and grandson Keenan, a nine year old bundle of energy, came to visit over the New Year.

With Barry here, I put out notices to start another group and within a couple of weeks had seven sitters. Jess had decided to come back, and bring her new husband Jason with her, but unfortunately the circle did not last long. After a couple of months I began to shake, internally. I would wake up in the middle of the night feeling as if my insides were in a food mixer and found it impossible to quieten my mind, so I had to stop the circle. I took myself off to the doctor who took one look at me and said...

"You're type two Diabetic."

I went for blood tests and my blood sugar levels were twice what they should have been, but within three months it was under control and I have kept it under control since that date. This did not stop the shaking, however, so I went back to the doctor and he had the cheek to say...

"Well I didn't think that was anything to do with the diabetes, I think it is anxiety."

I replied: "What have I got to be anxious about, I live in a beautiful house in the middle of beautiful countryside and I don't have to work for a living."

"Tell me a little bit about the last few years? He asked.

I briefly related the story from Fran's passing, told him my belief that, all those that had passed were safe and I wasn't anxious about any of them.

"Your spirit might know that, but your physical body and your brain don't, they will react like anything does if it is put under stress, and with what you've told me, it's no wonder you're shaking."

He prescribed some tablets which at first I said I didn't want to take, but he assured me that the quantity he had given me was not going to be addictive. They worked but to this day, on the rare occasions when I feel stressed, I can feel a slight shake inside.

When I felt better, I decided that the next circle was going to be for people who were already developed so we could carry on our progression, so Sharon, Eric, Barry and me started to sit once a month. Others joined as we went along and, although some did not stay long, the core is strong and today we have a settled group. I also invited Sharon to work with me on platform as she is the only person I have met, apart from Pat, that holds views similar to mine and therefore, neither of us will be saying anything that the other disagrees with whilst sharing a platform.

As the time passed, Barry was good company but I knew he wasn't entirely happy here. He wanted theatres and female company but as neither of us drove and the buses stopped pretty early in the evening, these things were not available for him. He would stay till Les and Andy came and then he would either go back to Spain or get a room in Portsmouth. At Christmas time I lost Finny at the age of sixteen to a mouth tumour but Dora is still trying to impose her will.

In January 2014 Peter rang and asked…

"Is it ok if I come up for a fortnight in February to look at a few houses?"

He found a small bungalow in the same village and moved here in May of that year.

Dominic went to Drama school in September, after already having a speaking part in an Oscar winning film 'The Imitation Game'. Les, Andy and I went to see it in 2015, and Les timed his screen appearances at 1 minute 33 seconds, but hey it's a good start. Les and Andy arrived in September, with their cat Dobby, and have been here nearly two years now. Andy has turned the garage into his workshop as he loves woodwork and we have a new grandfather clock and settle in the hallway. Les is doing a degree in Anthropology at Lampeter University and Barry moved back to Portsmouth, close to all the amenities he wanted, but he still has a holiday with us here each year.

Stepson Andrew married his Thai girlfriend Nappa, on Christmas Day 2015 in Thailand, and they have bought a nice house with coffee shop and orchard up in the hills. Napa has left the ship but Andrew is still there working to fund it all. Napa goes out to the ship several times each year and Andrew spends all his holiday time with her. I pray and think it will work out well for them. Stu and Fay are very happy together and still teaching, while Chrissie still makes us laugh with all of her crazy adventures. Joshua got his degree in Geography and is now teaching in Portsmouth and Dom is just starting his second year in Drama school. And then there is me...

Sharon and I still work on the platforms of Welsh spiritualist churches, and I am still trying to get the message across that: "It is not all about the message, but more about the progression of the spirit." Not a day goes by when I don't think of my beautiful Frances and her wonderful smile and realise how lucky I've been.

Of course this is not the end of this process for me, for I am still here and as long as all of you, and all your descendants, exist I will always be here learning, progressing and taking the whole forward. So I offer my sincere thanks to each and every one of you for being an integral part of my existence. Whether you believe the events in this book or not, I hope you may have gained some understanding of the reasons for writing it. I could finish by saying: "May your god be with you," but as I know you are all an equal part of god, he/she will always be with you.

"For everything good and bad that has happened, is

happening or will happen I am responsible. Exist in peace.

Prayer to the Healer

Lay hands upon my fading heart
Prepare my anxious soul to part
Lay hands across my weary eyes
To aid my restless spirit's rise
Lay hands upon my furrowed brow
Bring calmness to my being now
Raise hands from my tranquil crown
Whisper a prayer, lay hands down
Lay me under grass untorn
Yet know that I will be reborn
Leave all grief beside my stone
I am not there, you saw me home

EPILOGUE:

Since completing this book I have sadly lost my beautiful sister Lesley. She was diagnosed with pancreatic cancer in October 2017 and passed away on 2nd January 2018. I will miss her physical presence greatly but know that her spirit lives on eternally.

Joshua has had a change of direction, giving up his teaching job and becoming co-founder of Oaza Nadziei, a church planting movement operating in Europe. They are a Christian movement who believe in a God that speaks through the gifts of the Holy Spirit and a family of God's sons and daughters. Anyone interested in finding out more about this can visit www.oazanadziei.eu. Joshua is currently working with poor communities in Poland.

I have tried to write this as an 'I' book, in the hope that it will spark processes of thought without actually telling any individual how to think, but I will make one last statement using the word 'you'.

Whoever you may be, whatever path you have chosen to walk and no matter what position in society you hold, you are as significant as any but no more significant. Even the smallest nut, bolt, washer or welding joint in an aeroplane is as significant as a wing, door or engine, for without them all a plane would never fly. Walk tall in equality and know you are loved equally by the GREAT SPIRIT that you are all a part of.

A Question of Direction

It is said Heaven is above,
Hell below.
A flower's roots tunnel in darkness
enabling its beauty
to reach up to the light.
So must I burrow through Hell
to find my route to Heaven?

Derek Moore

NOT THE END